The Word Remains

Wilhelm Löhe

Selected Writings on the
Church Year and the Christian Life

Emmanuel Press ✠ Fort Wayne, IN

Originally published in German under the title
Sein Zeugnis, Sein Leben: Ein Löhe Brevier
Published by Detlev Graf von der Pahlen on behalf of the
Gesellschaft für Innere und Äußere Mission i.S. der lutherischen Kirche
Editorial work by Dietrich Blaufuß and Albrecht Immanuel Herzog
Copyright © 2008 Freimund Verlag Neuendettelsau
ISBN 978-3-86540-050-5
www.freimund-verlag.de

This English translation is published by permission.

Copyright © 2016 Emmanuel Press
Fort Wayne, Indiana
www.emmanuelpress.us
emmanuelpress@gmail.com

Cover Design by Meghan Schultz

Unless otherwise noted, Scripture quotations are taken from The Holy Bible, English Standard Version® Copyright © 2001 by Crossway, a publishing ministry of Good News Publishers. All rights reserved.

All rights reserved. No part of this book may be reproduced, stored in a retrieval system, or transmitted, in any form or by any means, electronic, mechanical, photocopying, recording, or otherwise, for financial profit without the prior written permission of Emmanuel Press.

ISBN 978-1-934328-12-5

Table of Contents

Preface to the English Edition v
Reading Wilhelm Löhe: A Portal (Manfred Seitz)..................................1
I. The Great Acts of God 7
    Advent 7
    Christmas..8
    New Year...12
    Epiphany...13
    Invocavit 15
    Maundy Thursday 16
    Good Friday 18
    Feast of the Resurrection 21
    Ascension 24
    Pentecost..26
    Feast of the Holy Trinity...29
    Church Dedication Festival 30
    Festival of Harvest 32
    Festival of the Reformation...35
    End of the Church Year 38
II. Our Faith 41
    God's Word..41
    Christian Faith 44
    Christian Prayer 46
    Church Fellowship 50
    The Church's Worship 56
    Regarding Creation 59
    Christian Hope 62
III. Brief Maxims from Löhe 73
IV. Johannes Konrad Wilhelm Löhe: His Life (Hans Kreßel)...............93
V. Chronology..105
List of Sources..109

APPENDIX
Löhe as Pastoral Theologian: The Discipline of the Shepherd (John Pless) 115

Preface to the English Edition

The Word Remains is a collection of excerpts from Wilhelm Löhe's extensive writing on mission, pastoral theology, history, and liturgy. Originally published in German in 2008 under the title *Sein Zeugnis, Sein Leben—Ein Löhe-Brevier*, this is the English translation of a delightful book that gathers his profound wisdom into one small volume, making it well suited for devotional reading. In these pages, Löhe articulates the confessional Lutheran understanding of the church year, the Word of God, and matters related to the Christian life: faith, prayer, fellowship, worship, creation, and hope. In addition, the biography by Hans Kreßel and the appended essay by John T. Pless give insight into Löhe's life, the context in which he lived, and his lasting influence.

Our heartfelt thanks to Freimund Verlag in Neuendettelsau for granting us permission to publish this translation. Stylistically, we sought to reflect the original book as much as possible, using the artwork (portrait and signature on the cover and flourishes throughout the book) they so graciously provided us. In the essay that follows, Herr Seitz offers a list of resources that can be found at Freimund Verlag, in particular Löhe's *Gesammelte Werke*, or "collected works."

We are also grateful to John T. Pless, who first introduced us to this project. In collaboration with translators Matthew Carver, Janet Frese, Michael Frese, William Staab, and Philip Stewart, we worked to achieve both readability and precision in language, taking care to express the richness and eloquence for which Löhe, who has been compared to Goethe, is known. Löhe chooses his words carefully, often intertwining his own with the words of Scripture and the poetry of hymns. With this in mind, we have added very few citations aside from those that appear in the German edition, which were provided by the author himself or the editors of Freimund Verlag.

Reading Wilhelm Löhe: A Portal

An Essay by Manfred Seitz

"Portal" comes from the Latin *porta*—an entrance, gate, or door. Since the end of the Middle Ages, the word has been used to describe an especially beautiful or impressively designed entrance to a larger edifice. What Wilhelm Löhe has left behind in his work and word certainly deserves comparison to a large edifice.

Many know nothing about Wilhelm Löhe or are only aware of his name and that he lived in Neuendettelsau in the 19th century and founded a deaconess institute. They may consider him outdated and not at all beneficial to the modern pastoral care movement or the doctrine of worship and practical theology. Yet those who truly deal with Wilhelm Löhe and what he has to say discover how relevant and deep this man is.

Wilhelm Löhe has left us not only a significant contribution to 19th-century diaconal work, mission, and liturgy, but also an extensive theological body of work. The publication of his *Gesammelte Werke*, or collected works, is not yet finished, and Löhe's use of language in these works has been judged comparable to Goethe in its beauty and in his profound observations. This alone is enough to establish that we should not only revere Wilhelm Löhe but also read him, as a Catholic scholar once remarked: "The Catholic

Church reveres her fathers and reads them; with regard to the Protestants, I'm not so sure."

Spiritual Theology

But how do we read this sort of literature referred to as "spiritual theology"? The concept is an unfamiliar one in Protestant theology. "Spiritual theology," which constitutes the substance of Wilhelm Löhe's works, takes up the scholarly theology of its day and assumes a great deal of what is set forth in it. It connects it, however, with "the life of the Lord in the service of the congregation," as Swiss theologian Eduard Schweizer aptly characterizes it. The aim of "spiritual theology" is a conscious leading to and growth in faith. It strives for spiritual edification by joining faithful understanding with Christian confession. You don't have to be a theologian to read Wilhelm Löhe; to a great extent, he writes for the congregation.

Two Types of Reading

Let us first give consideration to a point concerning the way we read.

There are two kinds of reading: lingering reading and consuming reading. People of the ancient and medieval world, where there were no or very few books, read slowly—repeating, pondering, and lingering over what they read. Then, above all through the invention of the printing press by Johannes Gutenberg (1400–1468), came reading for the purpose of consumption, in which lines and sentences were quickly skimmed. This is the way we mostly read books, newspapers, journals, and documents. The former, the careful and contemplative reading, which satisfies itself in just a few pages per day, is what we ought to take up again, apply, and practice. This is how we get back to Wilhelm Löhe, and this is how his writings should be read.

Spiritual Reading: Medicine for the Soul

In the Rule of St. Benedict (c. 480–547), one of the greatest documents of Western culture, we find some notable remarks about reading. Even though the culture of antiquity was in the process of falling apart during his time, his proposals led to a genuine culture of the book. Alongside the two main ideas of prayer and labor, he considered reading of the Bible and other spiritual writings as the third. In this, he followed the earlier monastic fathers who had said, "Let us take care to read the Scriptures; let us at all times linger in meditation on them." Benedict broadened this "taking care" to include books about the Bible and the faith which the fathers had left behind. In his Rule, he prescribed hours that were to be kept free for reading, for he understood the reading of sacred works as a means of healing for the spiritual emptiness of the soul.

Löhe Breviary

That is the purpose of this Löhe breviary. It is not meant to nor could it hardly be read in one sitting. It is meant to be read in sections, sequentially, and is well suited for devotional reading day by day. It offers Löhe in his "original tone," so to speak, and should be read lingeringly and with listening hearts. In the process, we have made some cautious linguistic adjustments to current German usage. [Likewise, in this English translation, the editors of Emmanuel Press have taken great care to express Löhe's thought, even in another language and another century.] This breviary also contains a short biography of Löhe and a chronological table, thereby rendering an important and relevant service to those interested in Wilhelm Löhe: we get his important ideas for the Church of today packed into one small volume.

LÖHE'S WRITINGS

Now follows a brief note about what is available and where one can acquire Löhe's writings. The *Gesammelte Werke*, presently twelve volumes, published by Klaus Ganzert in collaboration with Curt Schadewitz of Freimund Verlag in Neuendettelsau, must not go unmentioned. They offer Löhe's work in broad scope: from brief tracts to journal articles to his larger works such as the *Der Evangelische Geistliche*; his important liturgical and homiletical writings as well as collections of prayers; and an unparalleled abundance of letters. In addition, Freimund Verlag offers a fine selection of secondary works. To begin with, there is the compelling biography by Erika Geiger, *Wilhelm Löhe 1808–1872 Leben—Werk—Wirkung* (2003). Dietrich Blaufuß published one of Löhe's fundamental works, the *Drei Bücher von der Kirche*, in an outstanding, annotated study edition (2006), which is a splendid candidate for "lingering" reading. Also available are Wilhelm Löhe's *Abendmahlspredigten* (1991), his sermons on the Lord's Supper, which are at the very heart of his theology, his spiritual life, and his pastoral labor, published by Martin Wittenberg; and finally *Sehet auf die Innenseite…Impulse zur Spiritualität bei Wilhelm Löhe* by Heinrich Herrmanns.

It is enough if you linger, immerse yourself in these words, and read with a listening heart.

I. The Great Acts of God

A brief comment before we begin: the richness of Löhe's proclamation is best expressed in a short breviary if we follow the course of the church year and, accordingly, hear his message on the great acts of God.

Advent

Advent begins a period of preparation for Christmas, but it is also the entrance into a new church year. It is a season that looks ahead to the future. It is indeed fitting to behold Christ as a King of the future, as our coming King, and thus bring Him our hosannas. He is no longer as He was on the first Palm Sunday, and yet He is still entirely the same person. No longer is He clothed in the form of a servant; His physical being no longer serves to veil the Godhead that fully dwells in Him. Rather, His humanity is illuminated, glorified, and is a worthy revelation of His eternal deity.

His coming to us is only the realization of His presence, and yet for us a genuine coming; for we did not see and hear Him before, and now we see Him more closely and recognize Him more clearly. Blessed be His coming! Praise be to Him for visiting us daily.

Blessed is He who comes in the name of the Lord! He comes today and tomorrow and to the end of days. He will never turn His back on us, as long as we live! He is always before us. Hosanna, He makes us blessed in the highest! Say to the daughter of Zion: "Behold, your King is coming to you!" Where His Word and Sacraments are, there He is, there He visits His people.

The King is coming to you. He becomes your King through His coming. All Gentiles will walk in the light of Zion and in the splendor that rises over her! For the sake of my brothers and friends, but also for the sake of the straying sheep, I wish you prosperity, O Queen, Daughter of Zion, Church of God! If all goes well with you, then the world is enlightened and full of your consolation! But if not, then it will mean darkness in all the land!

Those who bless you will be blessed; and those who do not bless you, even so bless them. For you are rich and great and gentle in every sense, just like the Lord, your King, who comes, who is coming to you, and who remains with you forever.

Christmas

When the almighty Lord called the world into being out of nothing, the heights shouted for joy and the valleys sang His praise; the oceans of heaven and the seas of our poor earth poured forth; then at His command millions and millions of plants and flowers blossomed in the world as it came into being; in the heavens the sun, moon, and stars made their circuit; the air hummed with the song of the birds; the sea teemed with fish. And then man stood before Him, with his face raised to Him. Everything He created worshiped Him and what was written was fulfilled, that He had created all things for His glory.

But when the world fell into sin, then His heart pondered the restoration of what Satan had stolen from Him. He allowed centuries to pass and stayed silent in the mystery of His majesty until that night came, the night we now celebrate—Hallelujah!

> Until the sun burst forth from the abyss and everything paled before it,
>> the world of light grew pale in the darkness of midnight —Hallelujah!
> Until the morning stars sank,
>> until the angel of the Lord descended and all the spirits that God had created worshiped a human child—Hallelujah!

As He was ushering His firstborn into the world, He spoke, "All the angels shall adore Him." If the angels for whom He did not die worship Him, what then shall we do, the ones for whom He died?

We sound the harps, we raise the anthems, we fall to our knees, we sink down in the dust, we rejoice with the heavenly chorus in the Eternity of eternities: Glory to God in the highest, peace on earth and good will to men!

Today the fullness of time has come, today God sent His Son, today Mary—virgin pure—bore him.

> "Forth today the Conqueror goeth,
>   Who the foe, sin and woe,
>   Death and hell, o'erthroweth."

If there is joy in the presence of God and His angels when one sinner repents, how much greater must the joy have been when the One who was to call all sinners to repentance and cleanse them from their sins was born! Yes, heaven rejoiced and worshiped; the heavenly hosts sang holy songs above Bethlehem. But the Conqueror, about whose birth all the angels rejoiced, today He stepped onto the rough, difficult path He had to wander for our salvation: He humbled Himself and took on the form of a servant. A child like other children, crying, He lay in the manger, He who by His mighty Word called the world into being and through whom all created things are sustained and kept.

We stand in wonder before His manger, we bow our knees before this child, we fold our hands and speak: the Word was made flesh. The only begotten Son who is God from all eternity has become a man:

> O little child, You are God and man.
> You are our Redeemer.
> This body of Yours is the sacrifice
>   that the Father has prepared for our sins.
> You are the Lamb of God, who takes away our sins
>   and the sins of the world.
> You are my God and Lord!

Indeed, let us pray, praise, and give thanks. Let rejoicing be heard, let organ and trumpets sound, for to us a Savior is born who saves us from our sins! God's Son has torn open the heavens; He has come down to earth, He has appeared! Hallelujah!

This Gospel (Luke 2:15-20) serves as a modest echo, as earth's quiet answer to the glory of Christmas, the sermon, and the angels' song from yesterday.

The shepherds left their sheep to come to Bethlehem; it was more important for them to see the account that had been proclaimed to them than to protect their herds. They found in the stable at Bethlehem all that had been made known to them from heaven, just as they had heard it.

How insignificant is all that in comparison to the content of yesterday's Gospel.

And yet, for the shepherds the stable was more important than air itself, the little child greater than the pious servants. That night in the stable they did not have a sort of post-celebration, but rather a celebration in anticipation of the greater joy that awaited them in the stable. As ominous and frightful as the night may have been, it is more blessed in the morning at the manger.

It will become ever clearer to you that the heavenly appearances with all their glory had no other purpose than what we see in this Gospel: the obedience of the faithful, who hasten toward the vision; the subduing and salvation of their souls, as with Mary; the praise and adoration of the Lord, as with the shepherds who turned away from their herds.

The longer you think on this, the clearer it becomes and the more important it becomes to see your own need, and that is something very urgent and salutary: "If you know these things, blessed are you if you do them."

New Year
Circumcision of Christ

Whoever is attentive to today's Gospel and considers whether it deals more with the circumcision of Christ or with the name of Jesus, he will quickly come to this answer: there is more talk of the name of Jesus than of His circumcision. Truly the name came from the heart of God Himself; for it was not from Gabriel, but rather God gave this name through Gabriel. The name, then, must not merely be worthy of Him who received it, but also of God.

This most holy name—the name originating from the heart of God, revealed by angels, first heard and learned by the Blessed Mother and given to the newborn Savior on the day of circumcision in the Old Testament church; the name that has ever since been uttered by the Church with devotion, indeed with adoration, and repeated countless times every day and hour; the most blessed among all names on earth—may it also stand at the portal of this new year and be to us as an outpouring of fragrant anointing, like the anointing oil of God's high priest that ran down from his head to his beard and down onto his vestments. May this name be the first word that infants learn, the last word of dying tongues, the last sound in dying ears, the beginning of our eternal life, the sum of our never-ending hymns in our eternal home. In this year, may it be proclaimed day after day, may it increase on the earth, may every land be filled with its glory and in the end let every creature join in the cry: "Jesus Christ be praised!"

Epiphany

This is a day of great glory in Bethlehem, in the City of David, and in the house where Mary resided after the birth of her firstborn in the stable. The Magi from the distant East—wise, without a doubt; rich, as their gifts demonstrated; venerable, as their behavior and adoration before the blessed One proved; pious, believing, full of the Holy Spirit; a most honorable company, led by a miraculous star—they came through Bethlehem's gate full of joy and delight, in celebration and reverence, to the house where their shining leader, the star of the Wise Men, came to rest. We have very little knowledge about these Magi, which tradition thereafter sought to provide. How many, their homeland, their station, and other details have not been given to us, so we cannot know this as easily as we know other things. But we see and hear and know enough to praise God for the entire event and to extol with gladness these worthy first emissaries of all Gentiles who bring homage to the Son of God and Mary. We confirm that they represent us in praise and at the same time sign our own names on the list of those who praise this One.

The light of the Gentiles and Israel's glory shine in this day's Gospel, lovely and brilliant in every eye. God is present in Israel; Immanuel has appeared in Bethlehem. The day of manifestation is here! Countless days of equal majesty will follow this day!

We can call the entire period since the day of Pentecost a time of manifestation, a time of revelation of the reality and grace of Christ. It was then that our time, the Gentile time, began. And while Israel seems to recognize her glory in Christ Jesus less and less as time goes on, the choir of the Gentiles grows increasingly rich and sonorous, its day ever brighter, the adoration of Jesus ever more widespread, the army of those who confess the faith and offer praise ever more innumerable, whose princes are the Wise Men of the East.

And so we rejoice today, as should all Gentiles with us, in the anniversary of the beginning of the time of the Gentiles. We call upon the Almighty to make this time ever more blessed as long as it endures, that the host of believing Gentiles ever increases in number, that the salvation of Israel may appear as a light at the evening of the world, that the time of this world shall come to an end and be fulfilled to the glory of the Lord and His ancient, holy, blessed design. When our own life is at an end, ah, how good would it be for us to be able to say:

Lord Jesus, King of eternal majesty, whose kingdom we await, we wanted nothing but to serve You; we had no desire but to sacrifice for You. It was our desire to live for You, and now it is our desire to die for You, to be ourselves an eternal sacrifice to You, O Jesus! Amen.

Invocavit
Beginning of the Passion Season

Today is a day of repentance, and on a day of repentance we should not mourn only our own daily sins, but more than anything those sins that burden the whole land and all of time. But calling it a day of repentance is more of an exhortation to whom it is given than a description of what it is.

Who remembers his sins? And who joins together with others, with his fellow countrymen, to repent?

That one repents for all, or all for one, is a thing we do not comprehend at a time when love has grown cold. Hearts are dull, eyes are dry, hands are unfolded, knees unbowed. Wrong is not righted, not atoned for so far as it is possible; justice is not maintained. Everyone indulges his flesh; no one or seldom is there one who desires or strives to live penitently. It has almost become non-existent today.

It is as if it were shameful to appear penitent. All have sinned plenty, yet no one wants to appear ready to repent, no one is culpable, no one admits that he must change. Each one carries on as always, continuing to live in arrogant, sinful persistence, acting self-righteous and proud, boasting, bragging, and honoring himself.

It gives me no pleasure to speak of this. It is painful when one has to be the voice of a preacher or even moreso of lamentation in the desert! But is it otherwise? Can anyone refute what I have said? I ask, I await your answer, but you have none. If you were to give one, it would be more than you could account for!

But if this is so, then how can you speak otherwise on a day of repentance?

I want with all my heart to console you; but how can there be consolation when neither contrition nor sorrow precedes it? I know there are exceptions. I find them at the bedsides of the sick and dying; but generally, friends, I cannot say that I have had, much as I have desired it, occasion and opportunity to exercise the office of consolation. Lustful, proud, hard, self-righteous sinners cannot be consoled, can they? Shall we make a mockery of consolation? We cannot and we will not.

*Lord, from You alone come modesty, admiration, love,
and adoration; work them in us and in all
who belong to this congregation.
Be mindful of us!
Give us repentance and forgiveness of sins, for You must do it
all. All our striving and living and regretting is worth nothing.
Help us, and then may our eternal gratitude be Yours.
Amen, Lord Jesus!*

Maundy Thursday

This is the day of the foot-washing and the institution of the Holy Supper, the true, evangelical day of Corpus Christi. Behold the altar of our Lord and His holy adornment!

There lies waiting the bread, which we have brought to the Lord so that His body may be united with it; the wine already sparkles in the chalice, which is to be for us a vehicle of His saving blood.

Everything is prepared, and He Himself is ready to carry out the greatest of all miracles, to unite His body and blood with bread and wine, thereby sharing His humanity with us.

Even now He waits for our "Hosanna, blessed is He who comes," with which we go to meet Him at the completion of the miracle.

He is prepared to empower and strengthen the words of the consecrating priest with His Word, so that what He promised at the first Lord's Supper forever and to the end of days may happen, that these temporal gifts become eternal food and saving drink.

Who among you feels the dust on his feet? Who on this day of foot-washing hungers for the foot-washing of his soul? Who wants to see the humble Jesus kneel and to experience how God's Son washes the feet of men?

He who hungers, come; he who thirsts, come, so that you, who are bowed down on the evening on which Jesus' Passion began, may be comforted and made joyful by the gifts of His Holy Supper.

Up, my brothers, join with me. Let us take hold of the harp and raise our souls in song; as we approach the choir, gathering together for the Holy Feast, let us sing the hymn of singers entranced by love of Jesus the Morning Star, that dear hymn of the church: "How lovely shines the Morning Star!"

It is the twilight of the world and the last hour. At eventide it will become light when the Morning Star shines in the Sacrament, when the celestial Lily blooms in the Sacrament, when the Bridegroom, the high-born King, comes.

"Sing hosanna! Heav'nly manna tasting, eating, whilst Thy love in songs repeating."

How I desire to sing that hymn! If I could, I would set you all to singing! But wait, not yet. Let me now be still. Let me go to the altar. Let me go ahead you, praying, and meet the Lord there. Let me assist my Lord at His Holy Supper, assist Him in washing your feet. Then will the desire lay hold of you, and you will sing, as taught by God:

Oh, joy to know that Thou, my Friend,
    Art Lord, beginning without end,
The First and Last, eternal!
    And Thou at length—O glorious grace!—
Wilt take me to that holy place,
    The home of joys supernal.
Amen, Amen!
    Come and meet me! Quickly greet me!
With deep yearning,
    Lord, I look for Thy returning.
                (TLH 343:7)

Good Friday

If any day has the power to place the soul of man into quiet contemplation, into deep and reverent solitude, it is this day.

I want to move briefly and reverently through my text as through the streets of a city quietly celebrating the Sabbath light, not stopping at any of the individual houses but rather seeking an overall impression.

The greatest event that has ever taken place occurred in silence: no trumpets blared, no herald of God cried out, heaven and earth were silent, the sun veiled her face, darkness covered the land. And it pleased God to accomplish His greatest act in deepest darkness, to bring about His richest act of blessing unrecognized, indeed, even misunderstood. Nevertheless, the prophet Isaiah, my guide whom I follow, preaches; the holy apostles cry out, the hymns of the congregation resound, and I perceive the meaning of all this in these sacred words: "Surely He has borne our griefs and carried our sorrows; yet we esteemed Him stricken, smitten by God, and afflicted. But He was pierced for our transgressions; He was crushed for our iniquities; upon Him was the chastisement that brought us peace, and with His wounds we are healed"[Isa. 53:4–5]. Now I know what happened, and my entire soul bursts out in adoration and proclaims: "Praise to You, King of everlasting mercy!"

But the text does not stop there. The prophet leads us onward: "Yet it was the will of the Lord to crush Him; He has put Him to grief; when His soul makes an offering for guilt," then shall His soul not merely rest in paradise and His body in Joseph's tomb, but He shall also arise again in soul and body to new life, and the purpose of the Lord shall go forward by His hand.

Everything has changed!

The hands, pierced, that died on the cross have strangled death.

The pierced feet stand on firm ground and walk through the world as its sovereign ruler.

Just as everything was made through the eternal Son before He became man, so now is everything sustained and ruled by Him after He became man. The Son of Man is Lord of an eternal throne; ascended to the eternal heavens, He rules the world and guides it with His gentle yet omnipotent reins wherever He wills.

Now light falls from the eternal throne onto the grave of Jesus and on His cross, and Good Friday evening already glows in the light of everlasting glory.

O what rest for the souls who have found Him on His Good Friday evening. Light the Sabbath lamps, gather together, break open hymnals and Psalters, and sing hymns of victory and peace in the tents of the righteous.

Sing also hymns of the peace and rest of bodies in the graves.

O quiet, blessed Good Friday, O evening that followed great labor, O sweet evening sun after deep noontide darkness! O peace of Jesus the crucified, O God's peace for all sinners! O hope of eternal life, O glorious, blessed end of the Passion, of fasting, of penitence, of tears, of wailing, of longing!

> *Lord, be merciful unto us in Your kingdom.*
> *Give and sustain for us Your great peace*
> *from which all the joys for which we hope shall spring.*
> *Have mercy on us, O Jesus;*
> *grant us your peace, O Jesus. Amen.*

We will follow after Him, the Prince of salvation, and ever remain where He is. For those of us who believe on the Lord, this is assured, because we know that He offered Himself as a sacrifice for us and that with this very sacrifice He has perfected everything in eternity.

His last words from the cross remind us of this sacrifice. So we hang our faith and our hope on this sacrifice and do not doubt that, in the power of this sacrifice, we will find the fatherly hands of God ready to take us up at the end of this life.

Quite differently from Jesus, but nevertheless joyfully and blessedly in the power of His suffering, we will one day say: "It is finished!" Through these words, and in our own measure, we may and shall be imitators of Christ.

Thus we also say, very differently from the Lord yet still with complete truth in our own measure and manner: "Father, into Your hands I commend my spirit."

This mighty event, Jesus' crucifixion, enables us to follow Him. Good Friday ends; its sun sinks peacefully and serenely into the sea. The darkness of God-forsakenness is no more; solemn, expectant quiet rests on the hills of Jerusalem.

Tarry a little while, my brothers. After three days we will see all suffering in the light of God, and when everything is ready, jubilation will ignite like a bonfire, never to be extinguished. And the holy ones in Israel will be an example of how the souls of the departed, hidden in the hands of the Father, are certain of the return to their bodies and their blessed resurrection.

Let us depart in profound peace and endure the little while. Hour by hour the time passes, and in a little while we will sing of victory in the tents of the righteous, of how the Lord has defeated all His and our enemies and has richly provided an entrance for us into His eternal kingdom.

Feast of the Resurrection

Easter, the greatest feast: a day so grand and so festive!

Easter day is the king of all days, for it is proof that death and sin have been conquered, the devil's slyest plan destroyed.

The Lord is risen! He is risen indeed!

No other act of God has occurred on earth that has had so many witnesses as the resurrection of our Lord—so many faithful, unanimous witnesses.

No other act done by God for the world is as praised and commended as the resurrection of our Lord. The earth quaked, angels came down, saintly bodies arose, guards fled. Pharisees and scribes could not conceal what happened with a lie; no veil of darkness could have hidden the splendor of Easter morning. Where is your denial, O world? He is risen!

Rejoice, you His believers, you with gray heads, you with youthful hearts, you men and women, you children in the temple: rejoice and sing to Him, sing to Him your Hosanna, a Hallelujah.

If He were not arisen but had remained in death's bands, what then, my soul? God be praised, an idle question! What might have been is not, for He is arisen. Hallelujah! If He were not arisen, then He would still be in Joseph's tomb and all my salvation and my joy would be buried.

If He were not arisen, I would not know that Christ is our Paschal Lamb, sacrificed for us. I would not know whether God accepted His sacrifice, whether I would be spared through His blood from the angel of eternal death that passes through the Egypt of this world.

The guarantee we receive through His sacrificial death lies alone in the resurrection. Without His resurrection I have no guarantee; I would still be in my sins and my faith would be in vain.

Then there would be no Easter joy, no Easter peace, no Easter hope. How would you like to live without Easter? And an eternity without Easter, if there were such a thing, how that would be!

It is all so completely dependent on the Passover Lamb and Easter, now and in eternity! God be praised, He is arisen.

Praise and glory and honor be to Him who has put our death to death, who has brought life and immortality to light!

Go and tell those who are dying: "Come, my people, enter your chambers, and shut your doors behind you; hide yourselves for a little while until the fury has passed by" (Isa. 26:20).

Go and prophesy to all the cemeteries on earth: "Your dead shall live; their bodies shall rise. You who dwell in the dust, awake and sing for joy! For your dew is a dew of light, and the earth will give birth to the dead" (v. 19).

Go and proclaim to one another: "Christ, our Passover Lamb, has been sacrificed. Let us therefore celebrate the festival, not with the old leaven, the leaven of malice and evil, but with the unleavened bread of sincerity and truth" (1 Cor. 5:7–8).

And may the Lord, who is extolled by all angels and all creatures, renew within you a right spirit, His Holy Spirit, so that you know to whom you belong and may live to Him, who is arisen, with upright hearts!

> So let us keep the festival
> > To which the Lord invites us;
> Christ is Himself the joy of all,
> > The sun that warms and lights us.
> > > (LSB 458:6)

Ascension

When the Lord had spoken these words, He raised His hands and blessed them. And as He was blessing them, as His disciples fixed their eyes on His hands and His lips, He was visibly lifted up from the earth by His divine power, lighter than a bird. Every eye, every heart, every hand followed after Him; they watched in amazement until He reached the clouds and by a cloud was removed from their sight. Then their hearts may have been like those of newly hatched birds when the mother bird flies from the nest, and they may have thought, "He will not come back." What is a nest full of hatchlings without a mother?

What is the Church if her Savior leaves her?

For this reason the disciples continued to look up, even when there was nothing more to see, as though they wanted Him to come back down or to be drawn after Him.

But He, although separated from them, did not forget them, and He sent them two holy angels who cried out with a loud voice: "Men of Galilee, why do you stand looking into heaven? This Jesus, who was taken up from you into heaven, will come in the same way as you saw Him go into heaven !"

Then the disciples were comforted and they rejoiced that they had seen His glory, the glory as of the only-begotten Son of the Father, full of grace and truth.

The Lord, however, after He was no longer able to be seen by men, appeared in His glorified power to the angels (1 Tim. 3:16).

Consider that magnificent chariot that carried the prophet Elijah to heaven, how splendid it was. And yet, what is Elijah compared to Christ? The chariots that took Him home to His eternal dwelling were thousands upon thousands, more than can be counted, and He rode in their midst. Consider the last day when all these chariots will be coming with Him again; consider how it is written that the angels will blow the trumpets and raise a loud cry. Then you will understand the glory with which the Lord was received by the angels.

For it is written: "God has gone up with a shout, the LORD with the sound of a trumpet!"

He triumphs over all His enemies. He has imprisoned prison and released its dead. There is jubilation in heaven as thousands upon thousands of sinners repent; He who is the sacrifice for our sins is coming, bringing with Him His reward, His spoils. For the innumerable host of the redeemed righteous are remembered by God and His angels.

How magnificent is the Lord's ascension!

And imagine those who were the first to follow Him to the throne of the Father! What a glorious sight that must have been, that this Son of Man—who never sinned, He of innate worth and promise who out of love for fallen man descended to grant salvation—finally returned and sat down at the side of His Father, who had proclaimed from heaven before the time of His suffering: "This is My beloved Son in whom I am well pleased!"

If there is joy over one sinner who repents, what joy there must have been in heaven among all the angels and the elect when the Savior, in whom alone all sinners can be saved, returned! Who can describe, imagine, or even conceive of the rejoicing and the singing and the hallelujah that our Lord Jesus Christ received?

Not since the morning stars praised the Lord in His creation has there been a day like Ascension. It is the greatest feast; indeed, on that day in heaven a continuous feast began whose hymns of praise have not yet been stilled nor will they ever be. Yet these are things about which we can speak but little. When our time comes, however, we will partake in all of them, when in death our souls come to Zion and our bodies ascend to heaven on the last day to meet Christ in the air, as St. Paul writes.

Pentecost

Pentecost is the beginning of the gathering of the Church of God on earth from all nations, the birth of the Israel of the New Testament, the chosen people. For the disciples, however, the feast of Pentecost was a mighty step in their inner life toward understanding, will, and perception.

Only now did they understand Jesus because He poured out the Holy Spirit on them.

Only now did they perceive His divine intention because the concept of the Church came to life in a vivid and actual way.

Now they began to grasp the sharp division between world and Church, to comprehend the spiritual riches of which Jesus Christ had made them heirs, to be blessed and joyful in all their labors.

Only now did they grasp their new, apostolic call.

Only now did they enter with all their might into the will of their Jesus. What they had learned from Jesus had now come to life; what He had proclaimed was now fulfilled.

What began on that first Pentecost is still ongoing and endures until the end. The same breath of eternal love from heaven still blows, even if not accompanied by visible signs. The tongues that set the world aflame still burn, even if not in visible tongues of fire. We hear the mighty deeds of God praised in every language. The word of the apostles is alive in every nation. The multitude of those who hear, the number of the faithful grows and increases.

No one can hinder this work, nor will it ever cease. The Holy Spirit continues the inexorable work of building the temple of the Father and the Son. It is always Pentecost.

Our lifetime is also a part of the great Pentecost age of the world, if only the mighty wind does not pass by us unnoticed, and the flame of the Holy Spirit descends upon our heads and souls.

Do not lament that you did not live at that time when the Spirit filled the Church with the mighty rushing wind and flame, where nothing was easier than to live for Him because He was so near.

Neither rushing wind nor tongues of fire, neither good fortune nor joy, abundant as the waves of the sea, is required for His grace, which is better than life itself.

That first Pentecost was the birthday of the Church, magnificently and festively announced amidst tongues of fire and ringing from heaven.

But even a day of birth has its pains, its tears, and it is only the first day of life, which itself endures longer than only one day. That day of life encompasses many days indeed.

Our Pentecost began long ago, but it continues on. Pentecost will endure until heaven and earth pass away. Pentecost will endure even when heaven and earth pass away.

You doubt, yet I believe. Or do rushing winds and tongues of fire save you, does an emotional thrill inside save you, do signs and wonders save you?

You don't believe that, dear brothers. What saves us must be something abiding. The God who wants us to be eternally saved can never have salvation tied to something that doesn't abide.

May He grant us only what saves us, and we will have Pentecost day after day. Have you had enough of this Pentecost? Do you believe that God's Word, the remembrance of the Spirit, the peace of the Spirit, the fruits of the Spirit can be for us a spiritual springtime and peace?

Teacher, Comforter, Lord, Holy Spirit, teach us and preserve in us the blessed remembrance of Your doctrine!
Peaceful Spirit of the Lord Jesus, work in us that peace which the world neither gives nor receives!
O Spirit, You make all things fruitful; let us live and love and bear fruit for Your eternal kingdom!
Then will it ever be Pentecost!
Then will Pentecost be the crown and union of every feast!

Feast of the Holy Trinity

Today we celebrate the Feast of the Holy Trinity at the end of a long festive season that began in Advent.

From Him and through Him and to Him are all things: this we proclaim as we contemplate the long succession of feast days and the acts of God they announce to us, and we give all glory and praise to the Trinity alone for our salvation in Christ Jesus.

We know His steadfast love, though the length and breadth and height and depth of the signs of His love are beyond our comprehension.

But He, He Himself, the Trinity in unity, is for us a mystery worthy of adoration, of which no man can speak without trembling.

We confess Him, the Trinity, with the confession of St. Athanasius; we praise Him with Ambrose and Augustine in the great hymn of praise, the Te Deum.

We lift our voices to Him and draw near to Him, but we say again with Habakkuk: "The LORD is in His holy temple; let all the earth keep silence before Him" (2:20).

We praise the Triune God in the silence of worshiping hearts. We worship Him in celebration, and when the congregation has become quite still and properly conscious of standing before God, singing thrice holy to Him who is thrice holy, then the celebration of the Trinity falls like noonday light from heaven and the intention of this feast day is achieved, for it is worth far more to worship and be silent before God than to know of the immeasurable sea of His essence.

Reflection falls silent, the sermon ends, but the Hallelujah and the Thrice Holy will never come to an end. Amen.

Church Dedication Festival

Rejoice on this anniversary day of your church dedication. Rejoice that the Lord consecrates these walls, dwells in them, and in them shows you the way to the eternal tabernacle.

There is hardly a more beautiful day in the year than the day of the church anniversary. Where is there cause for joy and thanksgiving, if not on this day?

It is just barely surpassed by the high feasts. Christmas is indeed a greater feast, but what good is that to us—that the Highest became man and was laid in the manger for my sake—if it is not preached to my fathers, to me, and to my brothers, if we cannot go to the manger and worship the child who is the desire of all the angels?

Greater is that day on which the Lord bowed His head in death. But what good is that to me if His suffering is not revealed to me in the Word that preaches atonement, if I do not hear that He was abandoned on the cross for me, that I died in Him and am justified in Him?

Greater is the day of Easter, where men and angels sing their Hallelujah to the resurrected one. But how am I to know that He is victorious and has defeated death and the devil for my sake if the preaching of His resurrection does not pierce my ears?

What good is it to me that He ascended to heaven, and will come back in the same way, if I know nothing of His triumph and that I shall have a place in that holy city which is to return here with Him?

For me there can be no Pentecost without a place where the Holy Spirit can enter and work.

I need a Bethel, in which testimonies of the great acts of God resound, a place of rest and of praise for His divine mysteries.

Do we praise God that He has given us a place where His Word is preached and peace that can build up the congregation? A place where the ignorant are taught, the erring are corrected, where the faithful are led along the path of salvation? Indeed, it is a place where each of us is given what we need from the treasury of divine mysteries.

As much as I have encouraged you to rejoice, I do not consider it in any way superfluous to warn you against misplaced joy. Never forget in these days why you rejoice. Do not separate your joy from its source, that is, from thanksgiving for the church given to you.

Be mindful of this so that you do not sin in your rejoicing. I know, my friends, that for you, or at least for many among you, this is a necessary warning. I have also learned from experience that I cannot count on obedience to the Word and office of the Lord that He Himself has commanded you. So I will do today what Job did for his children after their days of feasting; I will go about in my silence and prepare sacrifices and vessels filled with incense, so that I may pray for you, that the hand of the Lord in Christ Jesus may turn to you in blessing.

Festival of Harvest

It is possible, my friends, that even a non-Christian or a heathen can be truly thankful for the harvest that God gives; for in all conditions of the soul, there is a degree to which the human nature is still capable of giving thanks. We do not want to despise any level of thanksgiving, just as we would not despise any level of prayer and ultimately must even accept the cry of the raven and the roar of the young, prowling lion as prayer.

But the Father wants to be worshiped in Spirit and in truth, and in order to have such worshipers, He takes His elect from the world, forgives them their sins, fills them with His Spirit, and enters together with His Son into their hearts, so that He might be in them and they in Him, their God who fulfills all in all.

In other words, He makes Christians of His elect, and then they can say that they are in God. Those who are in God are therefore rich in Him; in Him they are so abundantly blessed that they do not merely say, like Jacob to Esau, "I have enough," but even, "My brother, I have everything I need." Whether in poverty or wealth, every day they give voice to the Psalm: "Whom have I in heaven but You? And there is nothing on earth that I desire besides You. My flesh and my heart may fail, but God is the strength of my heart and my portion forever."

Such people who live in God and have full contentment in Him are not merely rich in God in the sense that God is their treasure and wealth; rather, even if they happen to come into earthly wealth, so are they also, concerning the use of this wealth, in God and do not turn away from Him or from His God-pleasing, blessed path.

They know that all their treasures are gifts from God which, though temporal and earthly, can still bring blessing in the spiritual realm through proper use, by the grace of God.

They have received their treasures from God, as from the Father of Light; that is, they have received these as good gifts and therefore manage them in such a way that they, insofar as one may speak thus of earthly gifts, may be returned to God. They bring them to Him, consecrated through prayers of thanksgiving, as a sacrifice. All their possessions are as sacrifices to God, from which they eat as from a sacrificial meal. They share these treasures with their wives and children and relatives, their poor friends and their enemies, as though they are sacred things. And if they can increase the kingdom of God through the use of their goods, that is for them a holy joy and gladness. For since everything came to them from God, they also acknowledge that the best use of these things is when put into service for God's kingdom and souls.

Therefore, they gather nothing at all for themselves for selfish purposes. They place all they have only in God's service, the same yesterday as today, today as yesterday, and tomorrow the same.

Their souls rest in God and are full of cheer in Him, and that good cheer is strengthened all the more when they can diligently serve God with their temporal goods. Their entire lives are led in keeping with the words of verse 33 of our text (Luke 12): "Sell your possessions, and give to the needy. Provide yourselves with moneybags that do not grow old, with a treasure in the heavens that does not fail, where no thief approaches and no moth destroys."

They place all they have in God's hands, and He remembers their faithfulness and pours out the fullness of His promise upon them. So they make use of the world, taking care not to misuse it, and thank and praise evermore in deed and truth the God and Father of our Lord Jesus Christ. Blessed be their thanksgiving, which endures throughout their lives and continues there in unimaginable abundance.

And so I say to you: if you know these things, blessed are you if you do them. I know that one harvest is not like another, that God gives plenty in one year and scarcity in another. I know that He gives one much and another little, and that not everyone can be compared to the rich man in wealth and abundance.

But I also know that there has not been a time of complete impoverishment, nor is one coming, that no person has yet died, nor will die, who has not been gifted with a certain amount of God's goods and gifts which can be used in keeping with Jesus' will. No one is so poor that he did not share in or benefit from the harvest, that he could not give thanks for the harvest and be called upon to do so. So shall the poor with the rich, and the rich with the poor, consecrate their earthly goods to the service of Jesus and rejoice that so long as the earth remains—to say nothing of how long we live here—there will never come a season, year, or day in which they do not reap and receive God's divine gifts and can then employ them to His glory.

May each one be diligent in bringing all he has to God, and may no one forget that this is the proper use and possession of God's gifts. For to the one who has, more will be given, according to Matthew 13:12, and he will have an abundance. From the one who has not, even what he has will be taken away!

Festival of the Reformation

Reformation and Bible, Bible and Reformation: these belong together, my beloved. They cannot be separated one from another any more than rushing from the wind or light and heat from fire.

We cannot commemorate the Reformation and forget the Holy Scriptures; every celebration of the Reformation is also a time of thanksgiving for the Holy Scriptures.

It is true that no nation on the face of the earth has been so blessed by God as Germany. It was in our midst that the man of God, Luther, arose, and no other nation can be as proud as we of having in its own language the Word of God, so clear and intelligible, so powerful and heart-rending.

Much grace has befallen us, only let us not conceal it. Let us fall on our knees with Daniel and, like the people of Israel at Ezra's time, acknowledge with weeping before our God: "To us, O Lord, belongs open shame, to our kings, to our princes, and to our fathers, because we have sinned against You. To the Lord our God belong mercy and forgiveness, for we have rebelled against Him and have not obeyed the voice of the Lord our God by walking in His laws, which He set before us by His servants the prophets. All Israel has transgressed Your law and turned aside, refusing to obey Your voice."

We have allowed ourselves to be led astray. God's Word is despised by so many in our day that many no longer deem it to be God's Word. If Luther were to rise up from the dead and see the unbelief that has torn into the Evangelical Church, which the Lord had once rebuilt through his service, I believe he would braid a whip—not of cords, but of God's Word—and he would strike the sins and apostasy of the German people, the sound of which would be heard beyond the borders of Germany! But his grave lies mute, our wretchedness hidden from him.

But the Lord in heaven sees it, He who speaks in Jeremiah 2:12–13: "Be appalled, O heavens, at this; be shocked, be utterly desolate…for My people have committed two evils: they have forsaken Me, the fountain of living waters, and hewed out cisterns for themselves, broken cisterns that can hold no water."

And am I wrong to maintain that a return to God's Word and to the Reformation is necessary? To be sure, not a reformation of doctrine, for there is no purer doctrine in keeping with the Holy Scriptures than that of the Evangelical Lutheran Church in her confessions, but a return and reform of the heart to the truth of this doctrine and the Word of God. Yes, it is necessary that we turn our hearts and lives back to God's Word.

The Reformation, my friends, what was it? We know what the Church looked like before it, but what was it really? Judge whether this is true.

I say, it was a time when the Lord went into His temple, braided a whip of cords, and cleansed His courts.

Yes, the Reformation was a cleansing of the temple. Or is that not so? Where now do we have all that indulgence nonsense, masses for the dead, sacrifices of the mass, works-righteousness, and all the endless supply of worthless trinkets?

That whole business was overthrown and swept out. The Word of the Lord drove into it like a punishing whip and put an end to the spiritual torment, the heavy yoke laid on by men and yet not humanly possible, but unbearable. The Word of the Lord burst in and overturned the chaos of self-interest, the marketplace of self- and works-righteousness. And the one who remained in the temple was the Lord with His apostles and disciples, with His sweet Gospel.

Reproach the Lutheran Church, however you will; you may hold her in low regard or see her as deficient or meaningless, yet this remains true: what holds us to her is that God's sweet Gospel and He Himself who entered on Palm Sunday are still with us in His pure Word and unencumbered, unblemished Sacraments.

Though we are miserable and weak, a poor, sinful heap, we may yet dwell by the quiet pools of Siloam and Bethesda and be restored.

He who began the good work of the Reformation, will He not also complete it? He leads His saints on strange paths, but He leads everything to a glorious end.

End of the Church Year

The church year comes to a close today. When we begin the next on the first Sunday of Advent, the first words read from the altar, from God's Word, will be the Advent Epistle from Romans 13: "The hour has come for you to wake from sleep. For salvation is nearer to us now than when we first believed."

"Watch," today's Gospel reading concludes, "Watch, for you know neither the day nor the hour in which the Son of Man will come." "The hour has come for you to wake from sleep," the New Year exhorts and entreats.

From what kind of sleep shall we awaken? From the sleep of false security in which we think nothing at all about Christ's return on the last day.

And what is this salvation that is nearer to us now than when we first believed? Christ, our salvation, the Bridegroom of our souls! Ah, surely we must be closer to the day of His return; we must therefore awaken and begin to live for that holy, magnificent day.

Our entire lives should be lived in anticipation of the last day!

Dearest souls, the day of the Lord will come when we least expect it. On that day, everything will go on as usual, as any other day. The sun will rise, quiet and new, to run its course. The earth will give her yield according to the season; the brooks will flow to the streams, and the streams will run to the sea as on every day. The people will go about their daily work and anticipate the evening; the old and the young will toil and do whatever is laid upon them. The children will hasten to school to gain wisdom for a long life.

In short, as it is today, so will it be on the last day!

No one will notice that the hour is at hand that the Father has kept for Himself. Then all at once, the light of eternity bursts forth into time. The shout of the archangel and the angels' loud trumpets resound in thousand-fold echo along the ancient mountains. Suddenly everything comes to an end—all cares, all rejoicing, all sighing and crying and working.

The world becomes silent: every eye looks heavenward and sees and recognizes in the midst of the angels the One whose concealed life is now revealed.

Those who have never bent the knee will kneel.

Those who knew nothing of true prayer will now pray and groan.

The dead in Christ Jesus arise as the earth and sea give them up.

The living are transformed, the perishable putting on the imperishable.

All who died in the Lord, all who live in Him will experience on that day a wondrous rebirth of their bodies.

What a reunion, what a scene will that be!

II. Our Faith

Since the *magnalia dei*, the great acts of God, were done for our redemption and eternal salvation, then we must also receive them in faith and walk accordingly in faith.

God's Word
Faith clings to God's Word

God's Word is revealed faithfulness and mercy; God's Word is God's gracious or wrathful presence, whichever is befitting. Where God's Word and promise are, there is also His power for grace and life.

Trust His Word. Do not stray from it. All else may be lost to you; all else may go as it will. His promise will never fail you.

The Word remains to the end. Let us look to the Word, be united in the Word! It proclaims, more surely than the rainbow, God's grace and the perpetuation of the Church.

It all comes down to the Word. We cannot do without it! There is no forgiveness, no peace in life, no hope in death, no salvation in heaven, no Lord's Prayer here, no Hallelujah there, if we do not have the Word. We pray for the Word unceasingly. For the Word we would give everything. Lord, keep us steadfast in Your Word.

God's Word is secure in the Scriptures

The Scriptures, although stemming from various centuries, are a united, non-contradictory message of God, while among the Fathers none may be found who remains exactly the same. Holy Scripture knows of no contradictions. It speaks more simply, irrespective of time and place, than even the purest of the Fathers.

We acknowledge that in the Bible, even in the New Testament, there are difficult passages, but we maintain that they are fewer than one thinks and are hardly of the kind of importance that would cause the general sense of the Scriptures to be called obscure. Either they do not at all concern the way to eternal life or, if so, are in no way contrary to the properly understood content of clear passages that deal with the same subject, nor could they be, for both originate in the Holy Spirit who does not contradict Himself.

Scripture is like the stars in heaven. Whoever lifts his eyes from earthly darkness will immediately see the great shining stars of the first magnitude and the path of light that girds the heavens.

Becoming accustomed to the light, the eye sees more and more stars.

Eventually, even the blue seems interwoven with light.

So to the eye of the reader of Scripture, there first come those shining, mighty passages, whose meaning is easily understood and undeniable. The longer we read, strengthened by that first light, the more other passages become bright and clear.

At last, we see more than just a Milky Way of bright truth in the heaven of the Bible; an awareness, indeed a clear, conscious perception of complete harmony within it overpowers us and edifies us.

So this is not merely a ruse but rather an assertion that proves true in every conscience, that the harmony of the clear passages of Scripture, such as those one collects for a children's catechism, comprises the analogy of faith and the proper interpretation on which the unclear passages are made clear.

On the contrary, it is doubt of God's truth if you fear that obscurity might be hidden in dark corners of Scripture that could extinguish the bright stars of the analogy of faith and simple passages that even a child can understand. Besides, Scripture has always proven itself in its clarity.

This much is certain: any hint of darkness that one would impute to the Scriptures lies not in the heaven of Scripture nor as spots on her sun, but in the heart and eye of man. And every misunderstanding of the divine Word by which one would mask that most wanton lie that the Spirit of the Lord has not spoken clearly and plainly has its basis in man's blindness and sinful nature.

The Word is like the Lord from which it comes: it is righteous for the righteous, holy for the holy, pure for the pure. For those who seek the light, it is light and it leads to a Church that knows the Light and lives in its brilliance and warmth. But for the perverse it is perverse, and for the children of darkness who forsake the Church, it is darkness.

Praise be to the Father,
with whom is the Fountain of Life,
and in whose light we see the Light!

No church holds so faithfully to the Gospel as the Lutheran Church; none maintains so pure a fellowship as she. Even a child is able to see this when testing church doctrine in the light of the divine Word; one will find that the most beautiful harmony prevails between them.

Christian Faith
How faith demonstrates itself and comes to know the grace of justification

Nothing determines eternity but faith—not works nor suffering, not knowledge nor feelings. It is only faith that gives peace and quietness, strength and steadfastness, clarity and harmony of the soul! Running about is worthless. Whoever counts on works, feelings, and knowledge, as if they should make him holy, is lost.

This is the main teaching of the Evangelical Church: the only thing that counts for man in God's judgment is that Christ intercedes and advocates for him. This justification for Christ's sake is the greatest treasure that man can receive, for through it he receives Christ and all that is His as his own.

Whoever does not have this justification by faith is poorer than poor.

Even if he were as rich as Solomon, he is still poor, miserable, blind, and naked!

Without this justification, which each of you can and ought to receive in this life, you have at best a false sense of worldly peace in your heart, but not the peace of God! Without it, you can neither live in peace nor die a blessed death!

I testify to this before all of you, that no one can come to this peace or blessed death by any other way than through the intercession and merit of Christ, nor by any other means than through faith and trust in this intercession and merit!

Once you have received this justification and through it have entered into God's sanctuary, then suffering no longer presides over you. And you will give thanks, for now that this most dangerous of trials has been won, you are either no longer subject to earthly cases or only those that, according to the Word of the Lord and the present condition of the world, must be!

But before you have won this case, it is necessary that you free your mind from the cares and afflictions of these proceedings and disputes and be concerned only for the eternal trial! And if perhaps you have not heard or reflected on this at all—that your soul is in danger, that your salvation still lies before the court, that the declaration of grace has not yet occurred—then even more so leave all else behind, even more so make haste to learn the holy doctrine and wrestle for certainty of your salvation, for you know that life is brief and uncertain, the strength of your life weak, your flesh frail and easily crushed!

Wrestle all the more with prayer and supplication for absolution and justification as you realize that you are heavy laden with sin. As your trespasses grow heavier, hasten all the more to Jesus Christ, that you may receive life and righteousness for His sake!

Most of all, hasten to Him if you already thought you were on the right path; for these are truly in the gravest danger who, without ever having been converted, without ever having turned from their sins to Christ, are under the delusion that they have God's favor and can die at any moment!

O eternal Judge of the World,
let many of these—nay, all of them—
receive the justification of life before they die,
so that when they die, they may enter into life!

CHRISTIAN PRAYER
FAITH IS STRENGTHENED THROUGH PRAYER

Prayer is as necessary for the soul as breathing is for the body. It is, as a wise man [J.G. Perboyre, 1802–1840] says, the breath of the soul.

When a body stops breathing, it is dead; a soul that does not pray is also dead. But I desire that all your souls live; therefore, it is also my desire that you breathe, that is, pray.

It is the Christian character to pray. This is so certain that the pagans, such as those in Tahiti, are in the habit of calling their converted countrymen "praying people."

Praying means talking with God. If we were to speak to a king of this world, we would humble ourselves, for we recognize the difference in station between us. We watch our words and our gestures, so that nothing is contrary to the reverence that is proper for a subject before his king.

So when you are talking with God, this must all be present to a much greater degree, for before God all the kings of this world are mere dust and ashes and unworthy to be called kings.

When you are standing before a king, you do not allow your thoughts to wander. Thus, when you are in prayer and think of other things, you insult the highest Majesty and are not praying devoutly.

When you are conversing with a king, you would not venture to carry on a conversation with others at the same time. Thus, when you are praying and during this time are distracted by earthly things, you violate the deep humility that is fitting before God.

Whoever is praying must always remember that he is speaking with God, with a devout, humble heart that is filled with God's presence. There is no greater honor than to speak with God.

But to which of the three Persons in the Godhead should you speak?

The answer: these three are one. Though they are three, not one of them is ever alone.

When you pray to the Father, you likewise worship the Son and the Holy Spirit.

When you pray to the Son, you likewise honor the Father.

When you pray to the Holy Spirit, it is heard in the same way by the Father and the Son, from whom He proceeds forevermore. Whoever worships the Father must think on the Son at the same time, for there is no father without a son. Whoever worships the Son honors the Father at the same time, from whom He is begotten, for there is no son who does not have a father. Whoever worships the Father and the Son prays to the Holy Spirit at the same time; for the Holy Spirit's work is to make known the Father and the Son.

The Holy Spirit works proper prayer. No one can honor the Father except in the Holy Spirit, and no one can call Jesus Lord except in the Holy Spirit!

So you may call on any of the Persons since you do not deny any of them. Or call upon the eternal Triune God in all three Persons. He always listens; His eyes regard all who pray to Him, His ears hear every prayer.

It is such a serious matter to pray to God in the Trinity that He acknowledges no other prayer than that which is done in the name of His Son Jesus Christ. When we pray to God in the name of Jesus, it is as though Jesus were praying for us Himself.

Whoever would speak with God must do so as he has learned from His Word.

What should you pray?

You may pray about anything; your conscience has no restrictions. Be it earthly or heavenly, you may bring everything to the Father in heaven. It goes without saying, however, that you are to pray most of all, first and foremost, for the Spirit of prayer Himself, that is, for the Holy Spirit. Pray that the Holy Spirit might also be poured out on you and in you, for without Him, what is the use of all that you hear in the sermons?

Whether you pray with your own words or with words written by others, both can be from the heart.

When you are praying by yourself, at home or away, pray however you wish, whether spontaneous or memorized; do not refrain from either kind of prayer. Practice both, and learn from the splendid examples of the Church what and how to pray.

The Church prays when she speaks; she worships when she sings. And the Lord dwells amidst her songs of praise with His Sacraments.

In these prayers she feels like the Lord's bride, rich in Him and through Him, but also rich through others. In her fullness, she remembers all the particular needs of those on earth. Wishing every good to everyone, she approaches the altar with petitions, prayers, and intercessions.

In doing so, her heart swells in considering that the Church throughout time is united, that the pilgrims here are in their prayers united and joined together with all the saints in heaven, that as they pray they draw near to the day of eternal glory.

Church Fellowship
Christian faith and prayer flourish in the fellowship of the Church and in her Worship

From the very beginning man was created so that he could not be happy alone. Let me say more: one person alone could never even be blessed. I know what I am daring to say, but I dare to say it anyway: consider an eternal blessedness, an unfathomable heavenly joy, and in it one person, only one, even if it were I myself. No! I would not ever want to be blessed all by myself. A longing for fellowship with other people is inborn in us, and this becomes most apparent once we have found the Lord. Conversion to the Lord makes the lonely fond of company.

There are many communities on this earth, but none of them satisfies our thirst as does one, just as each community is but a muddled vision and more or less a mere shadow of that one community established and instituted by God for all eternity. This one fellowship is the Church of God, the Communion of Saints. Our salvation is connected to the Church; indeed, the Church has been established for our salvation, and she will preserve and bring it to completion in ever richer measure in eternal life. Fellowship is love; love without fellowship is a dream out of the impossible realms of impossibility. God established the Church as the eternal union and communion of elect souls, with one another and with Him. In her is the most God-pleasing love, that which transforms all other love.

The Church is the most beautiful expression of the Lord's love, in which He demonstrates His own love for mankind and for His Son with unveiled face. God's most beautiful glory is love; in the Church He reveals love upon love, which she then reveals to all her members—to the living, the dying, all the saints—from now to eternity. In the Church we sing and speak of this glory of God, which is called love. In the Church, therefore, is not only our salvation but also God's perfect glory; both of these find completion in the Church. The Church is completion; and what is completed without her?

The thought that I extol is this: those who live in the Lord and those who have walked the path out of the body into eternity with Him—those on pilgrimage and those already at home there, those who believe and those who already behold it—are not two separate flocks of God, but rather one, one before the Lord, one in their own understanding. And what separates them is something transitory that deteriorates more and more each day: a weary eye that does not see, a staff that breaks, a body that is frailer than any stick or twig. What unites them is greater than what separates them.

"You have come to Mount Zion and to the city of the living God, the heavenly Jerusalem, and to innumerable angels in festal gathering, and to the assembly of the firstborn who are enrolled in heaven, and to God, the judge of all, and to the spirits of the righteous made perfect, and to Jesus, the mediator of a new covenant, and to the sprinkled blood that speaks a better word than the blood of Abel" [Heb. 12:22–24].

Here we see in a single glance the entire Church. Mount Zion rises before our eyes, the heavenly city of Jerusalem at its summit. Gathered there around God and His Christ is the Church Triumphant, which consists of thousands of angels and the assembly of the firstborn whose names are written in heaven, and the spirits of the righteous made perfect who walk outside of the body. And up the mountain to its summit, to the city, which is built so that the twelve tribes may be gathered together in her, there streams an innumerable host of men still clothed with flesh. Some are so near the summit and the city gates that they already shine with the dawn of eternity, while others remain at the foot of the mountain, still veiled in earthly darkness, the radiance of eternity not yet upon their foreheads. Nevertheless, they all belong to the city set on the hill, the heavenly Jerusalem, for to them, the living, the apostle calls, "You have come to Mount Zion."

They already have their citizenship therein. The entire focus of the Church in her pilgrimage is the other side; here she hastens toward it, there she finds her rest. She shares in the reward with those who have already overcome; with them she is an eternally united host.

The Church is one in all times. If the Church to which we belong were only three hundred years old, then she would have already been quickly abandoned, for she would be too young, a new church. And new and false (I repeat) are one and the same in these matters. But it is not true; she is not new.

Like a beautiful, wonderful flower, the Church has sprouted forth through the ages. From that very first blossom came the stem of a new one, again and again, similar to that first glorious blossom yet also itself a new blossom. At various times there are varied blossoms on the one flower; these are the various forms of the one true Church throughout time. Three hundred years ago that one perennial flower of ancient stem and bloom shot forth, and even now the world awaits the unfolding of the blossom of this stem in its full beauty. And even if envy should rise up against this wondrous jewel of the earth, what of that? She is still, by God's grace, the true blossom of the one ancient, unchanging plant, the freshest testimony of the one, unchanging power of the one Church of God.

The Church of the New Testament, no longer a church bound to one nation but a church of all peoples; a church that gathers her children together in every land as one flock of the one Shepherd, brought together from many tribes (John 10:16); the universal, the true catholic Church, which has flowed through all time and has her tributaries from every land: she is the great concept that is still being fulfilled, the work of God in the last hour of the world, the dearest treasure of all saints in life and in death, for which they lived and are living, died and are dying—this is what must drive our mission, lest we forget what mission is and ought to be. For mission is nothing but the one Church of God in motion—the realization of the one universal, catholic Church. Wherever mission goes forth, it topples the fences that separate the peoples from one another; wherever it comes, it brings together what was once isolated or widely separated; wherever it takes hold, it creates a miraculous unity that loosens the tongues of people from the whole world so that they have the ability to understand each other in all things.

Do not overvalue the visible Church, as is often the case these days, for this will bring dire consequences. Neither should you despise the visible Church, for this will bring dire consequences as well. It is even more dire that you do not despise the invisible Church, for this does indescribable harm. I need not warn you at all about overvaluing the invisible Church. One Church remains for us: an eternal, everlasting, universal one, united by God's clear Word, at the same time visible and invisible.

The visible Church, which has spread far across the earth, has splintered into numerous individual denominations, each of which has its own distinguishing name. One glance at the number of denominations and it becomes clear that not all of them can have the truth, that is, the full, harmonious truth. Otherwise, the separations would have fallen long ago by virtue of the power of the universal truth. The hallmark of the purest denomination is that its confession conforms to Scripture.

The Lutheran denomination has the defining mark of a confession in conformity to Scripture. Because it keeps Word and Sacrament in pure confession, the Lutheran Church is the well-spring of truth, and from her waters will those in all other churches be filled. The members of this Church stand in tranquility with radiant faces and sharp swords around the source from which all who are blessed have been made blessed.

Here is Israel's army and in its midst the ark of the Word and Sacraments, and above it the ark of the Lord. Yes, here is the holy of holies of the house of God, and when it is said, "May God send you help from the sanctuary and strengthen you out of Zion," sanctuary and Zion are here with the Church of the pure confession in which the Lord dwells in Word and Sacrament, more glorious than the temple of the Old Testament! This is the source of all salvation.

For here is unveiled, not piecemeal but rather as fully as possible on this side of the grave, the clear truth of the Gospel. What other fellowships hold as truth is united here with the truth. The complete truth, refined in the fire of centuries, which overcomes the world, is found here! Here it is confessed, in protest against every falsehood, that not a single word is surrendered! So it has been, and so it will be. The Lord who is with us will grant it! That is, quite simply, the reason for the Church. Do they disagree?

Let them rob us of the banners and decorations of the Church! Let them try to prove what they cannot, that our confession departs from the Word! As long as they cannot do that, the Lord is with us and we are the one on whose perfect fullness all other churches depend! Until then, we rejoice in what we have, bless all other churches, deny their errors, rejoice where they hold to the truth—refuting what is false and being united with them in what is true.

An impartial and unbiased comparison of Lutheran doctrine with that of other church bodies, in particular with the doctrine of the Roman and Reformed denominations, shows that the Lutheran Church holds the proper middle position in all the differing doctrines between the two, that it is in the middle of these confessions. At no point in its doctrine does it defend an extreme, but in all cases it offers the only possible unification and union of the distinctly opposite positions that have developed in various denominations. Nowhere has our doctrine taken a single word of Scripture too far, but in all cases it has, in comparing seemingly contradictory passages, arrived at God's truth in beautiful fashion and limitation.

Everything that the apostles wrote in their letters to exhort and encourage the congregations relates to the apostolic life. Yet there are three significant, splendid concepts in particular in their writings that summarize what we would call apostolic living, three concepts full of deep meaning for the Christian life that have nonetheless faded into obscurity: discipline, community, and sacrifice. These concepts are the very foundations of ecclesiastical life, occupy an important place in God's pedagogy, rest upon apostolic words and commands, are by no means *adiaphora*, are so lovely and sublime in their apostolic expression, such effective and powerful instruments, and embody so much else that is likewise beautiful and godly that we dare call these three in particular necessary to apostolic living and a holy congregational life. We would do well to lead the congregation to a better understanding and practice of them.

Empress Helen built many towers on the way from Constantinople to Jerusalem so that pilgrims could find their way to the holy city. In the darkness and wilderness of our ecclesiastical life, the little bands here and there who dare to meet together, to unite themselves with the good and withstand the evil, are like towers for the pilgrims seeking Zion. Those who want to join in the apostolic life can thus practice discipline together, maintain community, and bring God their sacrifices.

The Church's Worship

I know of nothing higher, nothing more beautiful than the worship of my Christ. There all manner of persons are united in worship; their faces are transfigured, their bodies and voices are made new, they glorify God, and the Lord does for them according to His Word: "Whoever honors Me, him will I also honor."

They draw near to Him, He draws near to them; the holy embodiment of this nearness and of His coming we call the liturgy. As stars around the sun, the congregation gathers around her Lord in worship services full of beauty and majesty. Words cannot express the soul's joy and heavenly delight for each of us who has the pleasure of taking part in the liturgy. Whoever wishes to worship the Lord, make haste, in order to be renewed while there is still time!

I'd like to compare the structure of the liturgy of the Divine Service to a two-peaked mountain, one of whose peaks, similar to Horeb and Sinai, is lower than the other. The first peak is the sermon, the second the Sacrament of the Altar, without which I cannot even imagine a complete Divine Service. In the Divine Service we climb ever higher until we reach the Lord's table, where there is nothing higher than heaven itself. That is my thought. Take it and consider it. Let it evoke in you an ever deeper and greater love of the Sacrament. Let it give you such a longing that you cannot be without the Sacrament, that the Sacrament would be your greatest earthly happiness, that after receiving it your entire life would be nothing other than a communion in the cup of thanksgiving.

The Church has ever taken serious precaution that those disciples who celebrate the Lord's Supper do so according to Christ's command. She has held to this strictly. If one of them deviated in certain matters, then he would be instructed, in many cases called to account. If, however, one of them was known to hold to a chief article only reluctantly or to an error in great and important matters, he was considered a heretic, as one opposed to Jesus and His Church and avoided as such, above all in the Sacrament. One neither ate nor drank in the Sacrament with those who erred in a point of importance.

Isn't it really something quite extraordinary, isn't it wonderful that on this night of Maundy Thursday, the One who on the next day would be crucified and from then on would withdraw from the world, should speak one command: "Do this!" and that from that day on and as far as the clouds reach, in every place and corner, there are not merely hundreds or thousands, but millions, millions, who obey this command? The God-forsaken One, who made no defense, from whom in only a few hours even His last possession, His clothing, would be taken and then His life, nevertheless wielded such an effect with His word, "Do this!" that millions across eighteen centuries again and again ponder this command and cannot cease doing it. Yet the moment they have done it, they immediately ask, "When will we do it again?"—so that one hour of obedience leads to another; indeed, it can be said that all of time is merely divided between the hours of doing and the hours of preparation for the next.

The words, "This is My body" and "This is My blood," are most holy, *sacrosanct*. What in all the world can be clearer than these words? And yet right here at the center of it is discord, for at the very moment when all souls should feel united in deepest peace, doubt enters, and bickering over this innermost holy of holies of the New Testament is at its very loudest, most particularly in the last three hundred years. "This is My body"—"This is My blood": then come the interpreters who declare, "No, that's not what the Lord means when He says that, because it's not His body and blood. It can't be. At most He means to say, 'This signifies My body, this signifies My blood.'" And in that way they make Jesus' words into the opposite of what He says. For isn't it the opposite if I say, "That is not His body," and He says, "This is My body"? Isn't it a contradiction, a denial, if He says, "This is My blood," and I say, "No, that can't be; it may signify His blood, but it isn't really"?

One would be tempted to say, "What impudence!" And this impudence, which manifests itself precisely in this interpretation, is committed in all seriousness by people who otherwise have the greatest respect for the words of the Holy Scriptures and about whom it would be said that they endeavored to let the Word of God stand and to bring every thought captive in obedience to the faith.

Regarding Creation
Marriage

Nowhere else is marriage so honored as in Christianity, for it is honored here as a reflection of the bond between Christ and His Church. Marriage is the glory and crown of the human race and yet is not a human concept, but the work of God Himself. This is an unwavering truth, that marriage is the glory of the human race and that the entire First Article has nothing so glorious as marriage, which God the Lord created at the beginning of time with and for mankind. The glory of marriage resounds throughout the heavens even to the uncreated place and is given by God as one of the highest gifts.

As to celibacy, the axiom should be that true wives only come alongside true virgins and true virgins alongside true wives. Showing honor and love for both states before one another and to one another will help us train up purer and more honorable wives and virgins than any excess to the right or left.

Fatherland

I love my fatherland, and I think I say this in truth and after consideration. I wish for the children of my people every temporal blessing, and if emperor and freedom, fleet and army help to that end, then I will gladly pray and work for this. But I also know that my earthly fatherland is a part of this world and my people are hardly better than others; indeed, I know that one can find more elements of ungodly character and lives among us than in many other countries.

Pious church members are also pious subjects. There can be no better citizens than true Christians.

Politics can never take precedence over the sincere prayer of "Thy kingdom come!" True love of country, which does not chafe but is quiet and strong, comes from throne of God.

The world is beautiful. I've said that to myself a thousand times as I walk through the greening meadows in the spring and listen to the song of the lark. But we Christians must be mindful not to speak of the beauty of nature with such expression, with such rapture, as if indifferent to the obvious groaning and sighing all around, of which our text speaks (Rom. 8:18-23). Just look at the animals with their mute, joyless, pleading eyes; isn't their sighing evident? The stark mountains and the naked cliffs, which are scattered out under the sky like old bones, weep with the anxious expectation of rebirth.

The Flowers

Tomorrow we observe the anniversary of the consecration of the church. Everyone is ready to celebrate. The beautiful sky, the splendor of the fields, and the blooming of lilies and roses put my heart in a most festive mood. The older I get, the more joy I find in flowers. They are so quiet, so innocent, and yet such potential is contained in them, for even when the time comes that they wither to the ground, they still have within them their seeds for the future.

The Birds

Today is Candlemas. Soon we'll hear the larks again. The sun has shone brightly and released the cracking ice from its bonds; two, three larks chirped and trilled about me and brought their long-awaited song, the sign of temporal and eternal spring, which is yet to come.

Christian Hope
The soul's longing for eternity

How often the comparison comes to mind, which I have read in Melanchthon, that in our temporal life it is as though we are enclosed in our mother's womb, while in death we are born into the light of eternity. More and more there stirs within me a desire to be born in this way like my sainted ones; for I see light in the distance and darkness under my feet, in a little while my feet are set in a broad place, and the light is as radiant as the day, for all eternity.

O Son of God, in co-eternal might,
O Son of Man, clothed in the living light
Of Godhead manifest, in power and glory;
    Lord Jesus Christ, Thou sole Desire,
    That doth Thy longing worshipers inspire,
For Thee alone, my spirit yearns in me:
No bliss I find until I am with Thee.

The field is golden, flowers the meadow strew,
The mountains rise sublime, the skies are blue;
In these the child of earth may well find pleasure;
    I too, rejoice in all of them,
    But, not content, I want Jerusalem.
Where Thou art throned, thither sets my sail;
Home is not home, except within the veil.

Angelic legions, in Thy brightness bright
Gaze on Thy face; my fathers share the sight;
The God-man's matchless glory is unshrouded,
    And from that vision, to the soul
    Unmeasured waves of joy supernal roll,
That rise in full and ever fuller tone,
Like ocean surges, to the Lamb's white throne.

Then let me go,—what further hinders me?—
To mine own folk, the Son of Man to see.
No glance will I, of that majestic beauty
    My eager soul would take her fill.
    Joy even now, and trembling, through me thrill.
I must away! Thou hast prepared my place;
My spirit panteth, Lord, to see Thy face.

O Gottessohn voll ewiger Gewalt by W. Löhe
(*Common Service Book*, 529)

Comfort at the Deathbeds of Believing Christians

The pain a mother feels when she bids farewell to her son, who is going away from home for a time, is no trivial thing. For mother and son are so intimately connected, find such pleasure in being together, and are so accustomed to being near one another that they can hardly conceive of being separated. Parting causes a great deal of sighing, tears, and grief. No one with a heart still beating in his chest would disagree with that.

Christianity does not remove this pain. As long as we are here on earth, all of the pain we endure, particularly that at deathbeds, ought to remind us that we are not at home here, that we have no lasting city but seek the one that is to come. Yet Christianity wants to alleviate this pain, and while all of life is filled with affliction, but also with comfort in the affliction, so is, for the Christian, the pain at deathbeds soothed through great, sweet drops of heavenly consolation. Thus does our Epistle (1 Thess. 4:13-18) offer comfort, not in terms of completely taking away all grief, but so that when the Christian grieves, he does not grieve as others do "who have no hope." The world gives no true comfort; only the Holy Church has comfort. Her comfort is true comfort because it is taken from God's eternal and certain Word, and the Church does not seek to comfort any more or less than that which God in His wisdom extends in His Word.

Yes, the dead live in God. God is not a God of the dead, but of the living. Whether or not we notice this life in the dead, what does it matter? It matters only that God knows it! Therefore, take comfort: it is not all over for those who have fallen asleep in the Lord! They are merely sleeping. He who by His own death-sleep in the grave sanctified our graves as mere bedrooms stands even now at the deathbed, calling, "Come to Me, all who labor and are heavy laden!" And when He lays them in the dust of death, He says, "I will give you rest!" and, "Here you will find rest." And if death is sleep, then each of the dead have the hope of resurrection. The great Helper—who raised up Jairus' little daughter, the young man of Nain, and Lazarus—resurrects the dead with far less effort than it takes for us to awaken someone from sleep. He does not require the glory and majesty of His second coming nor does He need angels or trumpets; for whatever He wills is done, and a mere nod of His head is enough to compel that great grave, the earth, to open and give back her dead. But on the day of resurrection, He will manifest His glory in inexpressible joy, coming from heaven in all the glorious splendor of His eternal kingdom.

Your dying ones are wrapped in His promises as in a shroud. This shroud preserves the body from eternal death. You yourselves will be cloaked in these promises when it is time for you to die. Whoever trusts firmly in His promise will no longer be terrified of death.

The Coming of the Last Day

Brothers, have you ever considered the work of the fowler? In complete silence he spreads his snare and net and conceals them from the eyes of the birds. After he has laid out his net, he goes off to a quiet corner, where neither he nor his net can be seen. All the birds in the bushes imagine that they are alone, that no enemy is near; they fly and hop about without suspecting anything, singing out so clearly. And when they are the happiest and have the least concern, the fowler tightens his net and the joy ceases. At this, we cannot help feeling pity for these birds. But when the world becomes ensnared in the net of the last day, we will not feel sorry for it, for it knew what was coming and paid no attention. The world may boast of wisdom and understanding, but it is even more foolish than the birds.

Oh, that I could take that reprehensible sleep from your eyes and awaken you to an understanding of the hope that blazes like the dawn in the sky! That you would seek to live a life of hope and join together with St. Paul in the resurrection of the dead! Faith and love without this hope are like the sacrifice on the altar before the fire fell from heaven. The great hope of Christianity must reignite us, if faith and love are to have their effect again, if there is to be an end to the debased, worldly character of Christianity, if the bride of Christ is to go out to meet her Bridegroom, who is more beautiful than the moon and more terrifying than the vanguard of an army.

The Resurrection

The dead in Christ Jesus arise; the earth and the sea give them up. The living are transformed, the perishable putting on the imperishable. All who died in the Lord, all who live in Him will experience on that day a wondrous rebirth of their bodies. What a reunion, what a scene that will be. On that day here and there parents will be standing at the deathbeds of young children. The children have died; mothers and fathers weep together. Then the Lord appears. He announces the resurrection. The children arise transfigured from their deathbeds, those who had first died in the grace of their baptism. What praise the Lord will receive from the lips of these resurrected children, how they will sing their hosannas, more beautifully than the children in the temple of Jerusalem at Jesus' entry!

Another scene: on that day the death knell will toll as on all other days; in the midst of funeral hymns and many tears, pious children will carry their mother to the grave. Then comes God's Son with the joyful song of the angels.

The funeral bells herald the day of eternity. There is stirring in the coffin—and the children see their mother's face transfigured and full of joy. The transfigured mother sees this and still greater things: behold, before her very eyes her sons are changed, their own bodies transfigured. Mother has found her children again and the children their mother, for all eternity! On that day, how often the story of the Jairus' little daughter, the young man of Nain, or Lazarus will be repeated! What a reunion that will be! No one will recognize his relatives according to earthly flesh any longer. Yet the greatest joy will not be in seeing one another, but rather the fullness of joy will be that all see Him, love Him, adore Him—the Redeemer!

I will be able to say of that resurrected body: "My body!" It will be a transfigured body, beaming with radiant light, a heavenly body. What a worthy companion this body, ruled over by the power of the Holy Spirit, will be to the human spirit born of God. How the soul will rejoice when it receives its old body purified, refined, and transfigured, and the power of the soul streams forth into the new body so that it moves on and over the earth, wherever it wills.

It is dawning over the graves, and the cemeteries are fields in which undying hope is blooming. May we stand firm in this, may the Spirit of the Lord seal it in us when we die; and when the ground yields beneath our feet, then may we be certain of this, that we will rise again like our Lord and that, just like the criminal who was crucified next to Jesus, our souls will live with Him in paradise until the day of resurrection. May the Prince of Life in His grace grant us such faith that conquers death. Amen.

The Judgment

He comes in His glory, in all the splendor of His divine attributes which overflow into His humanity, in the majesty of the omniscient, infallible, righteous Judge. All His holy angels are with Him to glorify His coming and to serve Him in His judgment. We will see Him coming with His host, the same ones who once sang, "Glory to God in the highest and on earth peace, good will toward men." We will see how His throne will be placed before Him, how He will sit down and in majestic, exalted tranquility prepare Himself for the last act of this world. All the nations with their people who are still living now gather before Him. As ears of grain stand thick in the fields at harvest time and await the sickle, so will mankind stand before Him. And now comes the judgment, a separation for all eternity. The sheep will be forever separated from the goats, the faithful from the godless. The Judge commands the sheep to stand on His right as a sign of His favor, the goats to His left. To the sheep He speaks a heavenly, sweet word, through which not only is permission given for them to approach Him, but indeed by this very word He will draw them near to Him like timid children to their father. Or rather, I ought to call it a command, which, even though with trembling, will be obeyed with delight! Ah, that we might one day hear the word, this word that throws open the gates of heaven, this word that resonates grace: "Come, you who are blessed by My Father, inherit the kingdom prepared for you from the foundation of the world!" But to those on His left, the goats, a terrible judgment of condemnation will be spoken, a judgment that causes us even now to tremble, though its complete terror can only be felt under the circumstances of the last day. "Depart from Me, you cursed, into the eternal fire prepared for the devil and his angels!" O Judge of the world, Lamb of God, by the power of Your suffering and Your resurrection, guard and protect us from that terrifying judgment!

Lift your hearts to Him, who will one day come again in glory. It is up to you whether it will be the strict Judge, who is no respecter of persons, or the Lamb of God, who takes away the sins of the world. Receive Him here as the Lamb, and so will He be for you in the land of redemption. But reject Him here—He who offers Himself as the bleeding, soul-quieting, peace-bringing Redeemer—ah, then He will devour you like a ravenous lion. His judgments are dreadful! Do you believe this?

O Jesus, Jesus, admonish, grant repentance,
grant forgiveness, grant faith
or the people are lost.
Jesus, Jesus! Amen.

The blessedness of eternal life is fulfilled in the kingdom of God; all else comes to an end at the gates of eternity or is changed, but love remains. Through these gates we enter into the fellowship of God, His angels and elect and all His saints, all of whom do nothing but love. For God is love, and whoever remains in love, remains in God. And because all His angels, elect, and saints are in God, so are they and so do they remain in love.

How wonderful to be joined in salvation with the spirits of the righteous made perfect, standing with them before Him who is for all eternity the beloved and adored One of the human race. Just like our salvation, the glory of God is made perfect in the Church.

He will make such creatures from us men that will marvel at themselves from eternity to eternity, from glory to glory. All powers will increase, like a seed opening up into a lovely flower and bringing forth fruit. There it will be a continual becoming. Yes, in the life of eternal splendor there will be at the same time the greatest rest and the greatest activity, a Sabbath rest together with holy, wondrous occupation.

How wonderful the Church will be then, a Communion of Saints! The great multitude stands in the light of the grace of Jesus, more beautiful than an abundant field of grain at the break of dawn. The pure bride of the Lord, whose body and soul have been washed in His redeeming blood, stands in silent expectation before her King. How great a love between the two of them! The Church sees His glory; indeed, she shares that glory with Him. She will be with Him always. Words cannot express the glory of the blessed eternity better than this: "She will be with Him always!" The queen of Arabia said to Solomon: "Happy are your men! Happy are your servants, who continually stand before you and hear your wisdom!" (1 Kings 10:8). What could we even begin to say of them, those who stand forevermore before the eternal King Jesus in His kingdom?

III. Brief Maxims from Löhe[*]

Anxiety

Faith prays mountains of worry into the sea.

Catechesis

Even if a thousand more explanations of the Catechism are printed so that it becomes a veritable flood, Luther's original word will remain the Ark upon the flood.

Church

The Church is lacking. She does not live as she should; therefore, she does not enliven as she should.

Even though the Church in our times is what she can be—and so, for the salvation of the world, ought to be—she is a

---

[*] With this illustrative selection of short aphorisms from Löhe, for which no claim of completeness is made, the editors have consciously declined to provide sources. [Freimund Verlag Neuendettelsau]

very small minority. She does not become a power if she is not small; what is not intensive is not extensive.

I exhort you in the name of the eternal Bridegroom to love His bride and be acquainted with her, the holy Church. She is a beggar above all beggars, but a queen of heaven for those whom He has blessed with His light. Who is more beautiful, more blessed, more holy than she? Whom, besides Him, should one love more? In whom does He reveal Himself more than in her?

Where is man's home on earth? It is where men love Him, and where, above this human love, God's love shines like the sun in Word and Sacrament. May your soul rest under this sun!

Church is the child of the Word and therefore can never stand above the Word.

It is a calamity that the higher notion of an eternal Church has been muddied for so long by so-called science; and while we studied, the enemy sowed tares.

The church became an "inn" which under a Lutheran sign housed a variety of people.

Our ceaseless habit of turning our Church into school, theorizing, dabbling in science, and acting with such childish pride by even sometimes cutting a new shoe or sewing a new dress for the ancient truth—nay, often for an ancient error—this has damaged the Church and continues to do so.

No discipline of pastors and candidates has been maintained. "Test the spirits" has been turned into "No, test them not." A mish-mash has been brought to maturity. How can conflict be avoided? We let everything count and are God's junk room.

The Church is not constructed or constituted by universities.

Community

A Christian cannot be alone, nor be content with just himself and his own salvation, because he has been born into the Communion of Saints.

Confessing the Faith

Whoever belongs to the Lord confesses; he confesses before friend and foe alike. He is not ashamed of the Gospel but freely admits that he belongs to the Church, whether he be praised or ridiculed, whether he reap sorrow or joy, profit or loss.

Diakonia

In our country, inner mission and diaconal service should originate at the altar, in such a way that there can be no doubt about our intention.

A little dishonor is quite good for it [i.e., diaconal service] so that it doesn't become conformed to the world and is not poisoned by the approval of those who see in inner mission not Christ's mission but only a means to a temporal end.

Löhe's Deaconess Aphorism

What do I want? I want to serve. Whom do I want to serve? The Lord in His needy and poor. And what is my reward? I serve neither for reward nor thanks, but out of gratitude and love. My reward is that I am permitted to serve. And if I should perish in the process? "If I perish, I perish," said Esther, who did not yet know Him, for the love of whom I would perish and who does not let me perish. And if I should grow old in the process? Then my heart will flourish like a palm tree, and the Lord will satisfy me with grace and mercy. I go in peace and am anxious for nothing.

Deaconess Motherhouse

You must have a home in the community to which you belong. For one thing, you need to be with those with whom you labor, for if the inner unity ceases, even the greatest work is shattered. Therefore, it must be your holy intention to strive for unity.

Ecumenism

The Lord will not unite churches, but He will unite people to the Church.

If the Scriptures cannot be the unifying principle of the Church, then there is none.

The desire to disregard the differences [among the Roman, Orthodox, Reformed, and Lutheran churches] is the origin of coarse misunderstanding and dullness and self-conceit, which deifies the beloved "I."

Perhaps the third millennium can hope to see that consensus with which people will then find precisely the least agreement where one appeals to it the loudest.

In matters of ecumenism ["union" in Loehe's terminology], the "zeal of the Lord" will do it. His road will pass high above the sick beds upon which the fevers of unionism and fantasies of love have stretched out the dreamers and visionaries of the day.

Edification

Being in agreement regarding the Sacrament and its praxis is, for me, how we build up the Church. What is the use of confessional quibbles? It would be better for us to be united in the Sacrament and the adoration of our Lord.

Education

Man has not only his present time, but eternity beyond that. An education merely for this time is hardly worth the effort to achieve, just as it is worth little to learn only for the hours of school.

End Times

Eyes on the goal, directed toward the day of our hope!

All the saints, whom the Lord wins and eternally saves, win and are won; and for us also, after hard tribulation, comes the joy of eternal success. Therefore let us not grow weary!

We look to the future, though it is dark, with complete certainty that it can reveal nothing more to us than what is for our eternal salvation.

We have everlasting peace in Christ! What is absent lies ahead in the future, and this will afford a glory which will surpass the most daring expectations of the children of God. Whatever is to remain eternally must unite past and future in itself. Whoever does that does not proceed by leaps, but strides calmly forward in keeping with his age and remains a child of the present and at the same time a pious reverer of past ages.

Enjoyment of Life

Enjoyment of life is the ultimate purpose of an age which renounces every saint and God Himself.

Failure

Whenever there is any failure, let a man not inquire after the proximal cause alone, but let him repent in every case. In order that all vain thoughts may die, so that man may understand that it is by grace and only grace that he is permitted to draw nigh to God, God must sometimes distance

Himself from him. When a man has been brought low, God then raises him up again and draws him to Himself.

Faith

Everything depends on the revelation of the living God and on faith. Whoever does not wish to believe does not see either here or there. Therefore give up seeing in this life, and believe in this life that hereafter you will attain seeing.

We have the general promises of His grace; we know that everything is provided in grace and that all our prayers are heard. Here, then, we exercise our faith (even in individual, difficult cases) and the quiet, hopeful lamp of faith does not go out no matter how dark it may sometimes grow around us.

A child of God knows that he fails and sins every day and, for that reason, when rising up and lying down, he wraps himself every day in the grace of justification. But he also knows that the faith of the justified is a power of renewal which penetrates the whole man and makes him capable of doing good and eschewing evil.

In this feverish age everything is regarded as indifferent for a Christian, just so long it has a great deal of emotions and inner life and speaks of repentance and faith.

A little while—and not a tear will stream from the eye, not another sigh will arise from the heart, and unremitting joys will enfold you. Cast aside sadness! Embrace in faith the joy to which you are called.

Trust his Word: do not stray from it. Whatever temptation, perplexity, or feelings a man may encounter, let him continually retain the sharp distinction between God and man, between God's Word and feelings, between God's faithfulness and man's opinions; let him stand on faith and press on with the unconditioned, unemotional faith that depends only on the Word.

Faithfulness—in Little Things

It is a hidden glory in the Christian life to practice faithfulness in little things, that is, in one's vocation; yet it is more difficult and more glorious than martyrdom. Martyrdom is aided by an agitated time, an emotional disposition, and it is often quickly won; it only takes a brief moment. But being faithful in little things involves bearing patiently the quiet tedium of a monotonous, elapsing life to the praise of the Lord.

Gifts

Blessed are those who have few gifts and dedicate them to the Lord. Blessed are those who have great gifts and do the same! May every gift be brought to the Lord as a sacrifice, employed in His service and to His glory! When you do so, you will find fulfilled in yourself these words: "Whoever honors Me, him will I also honor."

God's Direction

God leaves nothing out. On the last day, He will show you that He did not neglect you either.

God knows how to lead His own and always gives them what they need: for their desire, a burden; for their dignity, responsibility.

God's Presence

His coming to us is only the realization of His presence, and yet for us a genuine coming. Blessed be His coming!

God's presence can and should both delight and humble the heart. Man is in proper order when joy in the Lord and holy humility dwell together in the heart.

The Lord is nigh! All the sorrows of the redeemed dissolve into joy, all sternness into tenderness, all anxiety into prayer, all conflict into a divine peace which the world does not know.

Labor

Everyone ought to labor in such a way as to have his hand already on the doorknob whenever he should be called away.

There are no better laborers for the time than those who look homeward.

Whatever is begun in the fear of the Lord is well begun. "The fear of the Lord is the beginning of wisdom." The Lord lays it upon the hearts of His own in all that they do.

Do even the least work of Christ, and it is golden.

Sometimes a good thing is spoiled because the human tools which we have taken in our own hands are not worthy of victory.

It is possible that he who has encroached on another's office does no evil as such, but what is useful and good. Nevertheless, everything good and useful will lead to utter evil, thievery, and murder as soon as it encroaches on another's authority.

Labor whereof no benefit may be enjoyed, can plant a seed whose harvest may not be seen or brought home, and yet the labor may be done as if it counted as its own reward: that is the greatness of a royal heart.

Learning

He who no longer learns ceases to have ability.

It is my desire, as long as the sun shines on me, to continue learning and becoming. Nevertheless, I deplore the presumption of those who speak for science.

Liturgy

Liturgy is the poetry of the Church.

The true faith will not only be sounded aloud through preaching, but also prayed into people through prayer and sung into them through song. The liturgy then will serve the

Church as a new fortification against her enemies. It will be a holy shield and sword in the battles of the Lord.

Mission

Only a church awakened in the Life can effect life and blessing among unbelievers.

If everyone who lives among unbelievers did what he could to familiarize unbelievers with the Gospel, things would soon change, and the just accusation that not enough is being done for the salvation of unbelievers would be silenced.

Mission is nothing other than the task of calling, gathering, and enlightening Jesus' Church and sustaining her unto eternal life—a task which only the Spirit of the Lord can perform, but which He performs through human beings, so that in a certain sense it may also be posited as the task of the children of God, and indeed must be.

Pastoral Care

The pastor does not need to be a master of every new method, but he must be a master in the sole means of pastoral care: the Word of God.

The Pastoral Office

Those who hold this office are ministers of reconciliation with God, nothing more. And the ministry which they perform thereby is great enough as to require no glorification in the hierarchical sense.

To avoid such idle dreams, those studying for the ministry should be constantly reminded that it is not the podium of their instructors but rather the modest lot of a village pulpit that awaits most of them.

Praying

Every preparation for prayer is a conversion on a small scale.

Let everyone pray for an obedient and wise heart in those matters which pertain to eternal life, and only then pray for that which is necessary for success in one's earthly occupation.

When one lives in the Communion of Saints, intercessions take precedence. The petitioner comes to himself last.

Quietness

The Lord wants His work to be done in quietness. If someone lives in a state of agitation, when unrest comes in the multitude of business, its impact will be observed.

A wise man knows how to use solitude. What his Lord has done before him, he will also do. Let yourself be told right thoughts by solitude. Take them with you like a bouquet of sweet-smelling flowers into the quiet and sniff them. The first thing that you should take into your solitude is the thought: I, a poor sinner!

Raising Children

The primary part of a child's upbringing is prayer for, about, and with the child. By this his life is sanctified, and this is the first and most necessary thing.

The Sacrament of the Altar/ The Holy Supper

The Holy Supper forms, sustains, nurtures, and fulfills the congregation when it is understood, administered, and used as it ought to be.

Sanctification

Every justified child of God, moved by gratitude and joy for the heavenly calling of God in Christ Jesus, strives with all earnestness for the goal of sanctification which lies ahead!

O solemn span of man's life! O fateful span of time! A short time, and yet the mother of our eternity! If only we might use it rightly! One thing we should do above all else: live in such a way that neither death nor the last day can separate us from Christ and His Church.

There are people who throughout their lives never go beyond their limits and are never ready to deal with what for them is so difficult a question: "How far may I or must I go along with the world?"

They lack simplicity, which easily and surely skips over all that.

Ask simplicity how far you may and ought to go along with the world, and you'll quickly have the reply, "I don't know what you will produce with all your questioning and pondering. But my name is simplicity and I don't go along with the world at all."

Service

Whoever is most diligent to serve himself is an idler and a sluggard in the kingdom of God. Whoever expends and sacrifices himself for the blessing of all has walked the way of Christ, has best prospered himself and others, and has attained the holy, earthly purpose of his earthly life.

Suffering

Suffering should not prevent joy. Joy should awaken from suffering, and joy should bloom and flourish despite suffering. When God's Spirit keeps His Sabbath rest in us, no suffering will remove us from that rest. We have the promise of God's eternal rest and heavenly joy!

Thanksgiving

How shall I thank You? the heart asks. You can turn everything into thanksgiving—the smallest concern and the most bitter suffering. He receives it all as a thank-offering. And that is your blessedness on this earth.

We poor people of Dettelsau should dedicate all our labor as a humble wreath of thanksgiving and praise for His altar.

Truth

In matters of truth, votes must not be counted, but weighed.

Once, when I was a young preacher,
a blacksmith took me by the hand,
brought me to his granary,
and showed me his plentiful harvest.
The rugged man began to weep and said:
"Here you see the multitude of my sins!"
How often I've thought about that blacksmith
and his sense of guilt, which, when I looked at
my harvest which I was permitted
to bring home for God and His kingdom,
ought to have been a thousand times greater.

I often come a little too early.

A note from Philip Stewart, one of the translators: Löhe spent many years serving as a vicar after his ordination—a bit odd, for the modern reader. At this time in the territorial churches, a vicar was an ordained pastor who represented the parish pastor in various affairs, what we might call a curate or an associate pastor today. Fully ordained, he was still under the governance of another, who had charge of the whole parish. It is for this reason that the move to Neuendettelsau in 1837 was an achievement, though it was to a rural village and beset by poverty.

With the entire parish in his charge, Löhe was responsible for all the souls in a geographic area, the area of his authority. This explains some of the idiosyncrasies mentioned. Löhe could greet any child in the area knowing that he baptized him, for no other pastor could have done so. Löhe's refusal to perform a marriage ceremony for a divorced member wishing to remarry is even more striking when one realizes that this individual then had no recourse aside from the processes of the hierarchy, for without Löhe's written release, the marriage ceremony could not be performed in any other congregation or by any other pastor. Löhe's temporary suspension is the only thing which allowed the ceremony to happen in the face of his convictions. Yet the evidence clearly shows that Löhe was no tyrant, for his presence at the side of so many deathbeds is proof of a pastor much loved and who brought much Gospel consolation.

IV. Johannes Konrad Wilhelm Löhe: His Life

Hans Kressel

Löhe's life was an unusual one. He himself once said it was a life "full of exceptions." He was endowed with rich gifts of the Spirit, and then he had to prove himself within the narrowest limits. He grew up in Fürth, the son of a middle-class merchant family. His father was a respected businessman. Löhe's mother was a nurturing and caring woman who taught her children, and not least her son Wilhelm, to understand the Word of the Lord: "As one whom his mother comforts, so I will comfort you" (Isa. 66:13). Löhe's parents were pious people, such that love for the Church and the "beautiful Divine Service of the Lord" were awakened early in the young man's life. Although he was not yet confirmed, on Sundays when the bells rang at eight o'clock for the Sacrament—which, as was the custom in Fürth at the time, was celebrated before the main Divine Service—off he would go to St Michael's Church and seat himself under the choir loft, following along with intense attention and participation. Later he became the champion of the Sacrament of the Altar in the Lutheran Church of the nineteenth century.

After attending the distinguished Melanchthon *Gymnasium* in Nürnberg, Löhe was able to dedicate himself entirely to theology. He went to Erlangen, and here it was primarily the Reformed Professor Christian Krafft who became his mentor and led him to a consciously biblical faith. In Berlin, where he spent only one summer semester, he learned the art of preaching, mostly from F. Therevin. He became more thoroughly Lutheran through personal study of the Confessions of the Lutheran Church and the writings of Lutheran dogmatician David Hollaz as well as Luther's own works. As a result, he prized justification as the "greatest jewel a man can receive."

THE FIRST YEARS IN THE MINISTRY

After completing his theological studies and rigorous exams, Löhe had to wait for a position due to the surplus of young pastors at that time. Finally, the first opportunity for employment came as *Privatvikar* under Pastor Ebert in Fürth, and he could now be ordained in St. Gumbertus Church in Ansbach on July 25, 1831. Löhe: "I said, 'Here am I, Lord, send me!'" But his work in Fürth did not take long and gave him little satisfaction because the old pastor offered him limited opportunities for development. So he joyfully accepted a call as *Vikar* to Kirchenlamitz in Oberfranken. Here he could develop his abilities in preaching and pastoral care and dedicate himself to working with the youth, so that a "blooming springtime" might be awakened in the midst of the rough Fichtel mountain range. Yet not everyone agreed with Löhe's work and preaching, and his opponents were finally successful in getting the Consistory in Bayreuth, which was influenced by rationalism, to remove him from his call, much to the grief of a large part of the congregation. However, the Supreme Consistory in Munich gave him justice and called him as *Pfarrverweser* to St. Egidien in Nürnberg. It was here that young Löhe was able to gain experience and utilize his many talents. He caused quite a lot of excitement in the entire city with his sermons, which soon became the talk of the town. When he conducted services, St. Egidien was occupied up to the last pew, and many even had to stand. He occasionally preached long sermons, to which the congregation paid eager attention. Even the youth, who were not particularly close to the church, held this preacher in high esteem. Even today we can imagine the powerful effect of Löhe as a youthful preacher by reading his sermons from that period: the *Sieben Predigten in Nürnberg zu St. Ägydien* and the *Predigten über das Vater-Unser*.

In no uncertain terms he deplored the apostasy from the Reformation: "If Luther were to rise up from the dead and see the unbelief that has torn into the Evangelical Church, which the Lord had once rebuilt through his service, I believe he would braid a whip—not of cords, but of God's Word—and he would strike the sins and apostasy of the German people, the sound of which would be heard beyond the borders of Germany!"

And then he returns to the comforting proclamation of the Gospel in the great acts of God, preaching about the comfort found at deathbeds: "A person standing at a deathbed is like one standing at the sea as ships depart or lingering on the plain as storks and cranes take off. He can stop neither ship nor birds, nor can he bring them back. He watches them as long as they are visible; and then, it is as though he had never seen them at all." But, "take comfort, my dear ones, over your dead who have fallen asleep in the Lord! It is not all over with them; they are merely sleeping." "A mere nod of His head is enough to compel that great grave, the earth, to open up and give back her dead."

And with what power and clarity he depicts the coming of the last day and then describes the blessedness of those who remain with the Lord forever.

In the end, Löhe had worked in twelve *Vikar* positions before he finally received a call as parish pastor in the poor village of Neuendettelsau; the dung heaps in front of the houses offered a magnificent view. Based on his credentials and capabilities, he rightly could have laid claim to a sought-after urban preaching position, but he had make do and remained a village pastor not only temporarily but rather the rest of his life, thirty-seven years long.

In fact, during the first decade in Neuendettelsau he made himself available for a call in Augsburg, Nürnberg, Fürth, and Erlangen, but it was in vain. So he finally recognized that the task set before him in this village was given to him by the Lord of the Church, to which he then obediently turned. Now he acknowledged: "I see now that it is my good fortune to be here where I can be both busy and at rest. I wish to lay my head down here and sleep as the shepherd among my sheep until the almighty morning wind comes from the east." From this small place he was able to carry on work that spanned the width of an ocean.

At first his work was limited to his village congregation. He was an outstanding preacher with biblical depth, a caring pastoral demeanor, and captivating eloquence. As he would write in his book *The Pastor*: "A preacher shall speak in the name of God. Can he do otherwise?" He himself was such a preacher who truly proclaimed God's Word in its breadth and depth as laid out in the Scriptures. But at the same time he always had in mind his congregation's actual situation and their human needs.

He saw that it was given to the Church to "preach as practically as possible to the time and place and other circumstances," while at the same time keeping in mind the individual.

LIFE IN WORSHIP

Löhe was a gifted liturgist. Here he was in his element. Preaching and liturgy, proclaiming the Word, and celebrating the Lord's Supper were for him inseparably joined together. In the pulpit or at the altar, he could not "preside unless his breath flowed out like a flame." "It was the flame of the soul which sacrifices itself to God in the Office" (G. v. Zezschwitz). Thus was "a liturgical people" formed, which was admired by liturgical experts of his day. He was also very productive—after intensive study of the various liturgies—and developed individual liturgical pieces for his *Agenda*, such as the splendid conclusion to the Sunday Prayer of the Church, in which he poignantly expresses the fellowship of the Church on earth with the triumphant in heaven, as well as the prayer for the coming of Christ on the last day and the fulfillment of the kingdom of God.

TEACHER AND SEELSORGER

The preacher and liturgist was also a good teacher and *Seelsorger* [one who exercises pastoral care of the souls entrusted to him]. This man of great intellect could bring alive the magnificence of the Lutheran catechism as a "golden jewel" and a true "lay-Bible" for young and old alike. His confirmation instruction was exemplary; his Bible studies for the confirmed youth on Sunday afternoons delighted the adults of the congregation as well. The subject of baptism moved him so much that occasionally he would embrace a child on the street who wanted to shake the pastor's hand and ask, "Are you baptized?" If the child then looked up, startled and in bashful silence, he would say, "Yes, you are baptized! I baptized you myself! Now go home and have your godparents and parents tell you what your baptism was all about."

Löhe practiced care of souls above all in Confession and Absolution, both in private confession and in the general public confession, and at the bedside of the sick and dying. Löhe did not hold the general confession in low regard. He wanted to know that this form of confession was rightly preserved, and he held impressive confessional lessons in the confession services. But the reintroduction of private confession lay close to Löhe's heart. In the end, most of his members confessed privately. Löhe often acknowledged: "Days of confession are blessed days, not only because I myself confess, but also because I experience so often and so deeply how God's grace penetrates my parishioners." Prof. G. v. Zezschwitz, a man who himself confessed to Löhe, described him as father confessor: "…This combination of a holy earnestness and paternal goodness, this wonderful subjection of his own will and judgment, this renunciation of any dominion over the souls, according to God's light and law, in order to dispense to each one according to his need the comfort of grace and to admonish each to an amended life: this is how we know him, and whoever does not know him thus has not learned to know him rightly."

Attending the Dying

Löhe carried out his *Seelsorger* duties at the bedsides of the sick and dying tirelessly. It was a rare occurrence that someone in his congregation died without the pastor being called to strengthen him with Word and prayer and with Holy Communion, blessing him and staying with him in the final moments. How often Löhe was given the opportunity to help an anxious soul conquer the fear of death and give him wings for a blessed return home. He could cheer the despairing: "Fear not, it's nothing but a little death." He greeted a dying woman: "The Lord is near!" and as she repeated the greeting, he continued, "The Bridegroom is coming; go to him in good health!" Or at the hospital bed of a dying deaconess he prayed, "Jesus of Nazareth, You who know what it is to die, stretch out Your strong hand now to Your maidservant." He once offered this judgment: "The Dettelsauers know perhaps not how to live well, but certainly how to die well." On several occasions in praying for the sick, both physically and spiritually sick, he received extraordinary answers to prayer, perhaps similar to Blumhardt.

Stirred to Mission Work

As strenuously as he labored in his village congregation, he still found time to extend his work far beyond the borders of his congregation. Convinced that "mission is nothing but the one Church of God in motion," he established the Native American mission in North America. He was aware of the special difficulties imposed on this mission from the start; the greatest hindrance with regards to Christian faith for the Native Americans was the unchristian treatment from the white men they had endured for such a long time. As a new uprising of the warlike Sioux tribe flared up against the unjust oppression by the whites, Dettelsau missionary Moritz Bräuninger was killed on July 23, 1860, and not long after that the Native American mission had to be closed. But the "blood of the martyr" would here later become "the seed of the Church." The Neuendettelsau mission would continue its work in New Guinea and other lands.

Along with the mission work in North America, Löhe wanted to support the German Lutherans there by means of diaspora care and encouragement. When the cry for help from the American Pastor Wynecken reached him, he issued a fiery appeal to the congregations in the Nördlinger Sunday newspaper: "Our brothers are wandering in the wilderness of North America without food for the soul. We have our hands in our laps and forget to help....Up, brothers, let us help as much as we can! I ask you for Christ's sake, lend a hand, come together quickly! Don't think too long on it! Hurry! There are immortal souls to be saved."

In his own parsonage, Löhe himself immediately began training two young men who had come to him so that they were able to help out to some extent as teacher and pastor, and he sent them out. That was the beginning of the American diaspora mission, which he further expanded through the founding of colonies like Frankenmuth, Frankenlust, Frankentrost, and Frankenhilf [translated literally, respectively, as the courage, desire, comfort, and help of the Franconians]. The emigrants and the accompanying emissaries, or "emergency helpers," sent by Löhe are also responsible for the enduring and present significance of Löhe in American Lutheranism. In some parts of America, Löhe is today better known and more widely read than in his home country.

From the microcosm of Löhe's training arose the Missions and Diaspora Seminary, at which missionaries and pastors were educated until 1985.

Inner Mission

For Löhe the "inner" mission was inseparable from the "outer" mission. He stated this in his seminal essay on "Inner Mission" held at Nürnberg in 1850: "Observation of the present condition of the Church has inclined us to divide the world no longer into two spheres, but rather three. In the first dwell the unbaptized; in the second and third, the baptized. In the second are the baptized who, faithful to the Word in some measure, allow themselves to be taught the way of eternal life; but in the third are those who have either fallen away or are in danger of doing so, whose piety and therefore morality degenerate more and more. And now what the Church must do in genuine love for the salvation of this most miserable third group of people, after the manner of the Savior of sinners, we would preferably designate, although not entirely accurately, with the name 'Inner Mission.'"

In order to be able to carry out the work of inner mission and Christian labors of love in general, Löhe restored the office of the female diaconate, for "because the entirety of the person is comprised of both body and soul, it is impossible for inner mission to abstain from acts and deeds of physical mercy."

Since his original plan was to educate female laborers from the various congregations and then send them back to their home congregations, then it would be necessary for them to have their own deaconess institute—a motherhouse for the sisters. He wanted to ensure that they were uniquely formed: "…a deaconess should be able to and should do the least and the greatest, not being ashamed of the least nor demeaning the highest labor of women. With her feet in the dung and dust of lowly work, her hands on the harp, her head in the sunlight of prayerful devotion and understanding of Jesus; this is how I would picture her as the frontispiece. And underneath I would write, 'She is able to do everything, working, playing, singing praise.'" Since then Löhe's deaconess institute has grown into the large Diakonie Neuendettelsau with around 6000 employees, of whom only a small part are identified as deaconesses.

Distinctive and Ecumenical Lutheranism

In all of this, Löhe was the untiring champion of a distinctive and ecumenical Lutheranism and, for the sake of his beloved Lutheran Church and Lutheran confession and practice, he did not shy away from difficult situations. At that time there were still remnants of "dry faith-based-on-reason" (rationalism) in the Bavarian *Landeskirche* [territorial church] and elsewhere. An appropriate understanding was lacking of the differences between the Lutheran and Reformed churches, especially concerning the doctrine of Holy Communion. Regarding this, Löhe had long contended for clarification and purification. He fought against every "mingling of Holy Communion" and strove for a genuine church discipline based on brotherly love. Doctrine and discipline are indispensable to the Church. No doubt there were like-minded people who stood with him, those whom he had gathered together in the *Gesellschaft für Innere Mission im Sinne der lutherische Kirche* [Society for Inner Mission in the Manner of the Lutheran Church]. But he found no support from his old friends among the Lutheran faculty at Erlangen, to whom he appeared too narrow.

Several times he was to the point of transferring to a Lutheran free church. In 1860 he was suspended from the clerical office because he refused to perform a marriage for a divorced member of the congregation. But then Löhe decided to remain in his church nonetheless and, despite all the difficulties, to continue to work here according to the Lutheran way and strive for an "apostolic life" in the congregations.

LÖHE AS AUTHOR

Löhe served the Evangelical Lutheran Church as a scholar and author, but his reach extended beyond. There are few professors in academic positions who have produced as much with their pens as this village pastor. His *Agenda for Christian Congregations of the Lutheran Faith* reveals the depth of his scholarly research. He produced devotional books and individual sermons. His tracts, such as the outstanding little paper, *On the Divine Word, as the Light which Leads to Peace*, had an effect that is not to be underestimated. He also wrote prayer books such as *Seed-Grains*, *Rauchopfer*, and others. His *Confession- and Communion-Book*, his *House-, School-, and Church-Book* in particular, and, not to be forgotten, his renowned *Three Books about the Church* as well as his *Proposal of a Union of Lutheran Christians for Apostolic Life* are important writings, most of which are found in the *Collected Works*.

He offered pastors a book on pastoral theology called *The Pastor*. Concerning practical theology, he did not forget church history and wrote his *Remembrances from the Reformation History of Franconia*. Some sixty larger and smaller writings and books are available. Löhe served the church through his writing. In his books and tracts he also showed his expertise as a classicist and master of form. But for all the variety of his work, he always kept a simple faith, tied closely to Word and Sacrament. For him the Word of God was, as he stated in one of his tracts, the one light that leads to true peace.

He wanted to live in Holy Communion as "a day laborer from one meal to the next." Next to the mystery of the divine Trinity he viewed Holy Communion as the greatest mystery and saw in its celebration the gates of paradise already open. His *Sermons on Holy Communion*, published in 1991, convey this. Thanks to the redemption through Jesus Christ and sanctification and strengthening by the Holy Spirit, Löhe was also able to carry the cross laid on him, in particular the early death of his beloved wife, but also the actual poverty of his village pastorate. In addition, he had a number of health problems. Löhe nevertheless persevered in faith to the end and extolled the grace of the Lord which "is powerful in the weak."

On New Year's Day 1872, Löhe suffered a severe stroke and on the next day was led, as in a dream, through the gates of death. He had once said, as though in anticipation of his own end, at a wedding address in connection with Exodus 14:14, that even a death without consciousness would be a blessed end, where only the inner life in Christ is present, and thus was it granted to him: "The Lord will fight for you; you need only to be still." Before he was carried out to the cemetery, where he wanted to sleep until the Lord came to call him, the words of the prophet were read over his open coffin:

"And those who are wise shall shine like the brightness of the sky above; and those who turn many to righteousness, like the stars forever and ever."

And: "But go your way till the end. And you shall rest and shall stand in your allotted place at the end of the days." (Dan. 12:3, 13)

V. Chronology

1808	February 21: Löhe's birth in Fürth
1826-1831	Theological studies
1831	July 25: Ordination to the Office of the Holy Ministry in Ansbach at St. Gumbertus
1831-1837	*Vikar* in Kirchenlamitz, *Pfarrvertretung* in Nürnberg, Altdorf, Bertholdsdorf, Merkendorf, and other places
1837	August 1: Installation as pastor of Neuendettelsau
1841	Pastor Wynecken's call for help for fellow Lutherans in North America—taken up intensively by Löhe
	Beginning of the work of the Mission Society (formally established in 1849)
	July: Adam Ernst (Oettingen)—first pastoral helper (*Sendling*) for the Lutheran mission with Löhe; Fall 1841: Georg Burger (Nördlingen) joins in as the second
	July 11: Sending of A. Ernst and G. Burger to North America. Until 1925 (when the sending of missionaries to North America came to an end) a total of 320 workers were sent from Neuendettelsau to North America
	January: Publication of the "Kirchlichen Mitteilungen aus und ueber Nordamerika" ["Church Reports from and about North America"] (circulation the first year: 8000, 12 issues annually)

1843	November 24: Death of Löhe's wife, Helene
1844	Expansion of education and training opportunities for Lutheran missionaries (in Augsburg, Nürnberg, Auernheim)
1845	April 20: Embarkation to North America of the first Franconian colonists (with Pastor Crämer) as Lutheran mission congregations
	Founding of Frankenmuth in Michigan and beginning of the Native American mission
	School for Native American children in Frankenmuth
	Friedrich Bauer—head of the Lutheran mission school in Nürnberg until 1853, in Neuendettelsau until 1874
	September 24: Löhe's "Call from the Homeland to the German Lutheran Church of North America"
1846	October 10: Founding of the Lutheran Seminary in Fort Wayne by the Franconian settlers
	Christmas: The first Native American baptism (Abuiquam – "Abraham" – and his two sisters, Magdalena and Anna)
1847	April: Founding of the Synod of Missouri, Ohio, and Other States—resulting from various church conflicts and clarification processes
	Founding of the second and third German Lutheran colonies: Frankentrost and Frankenlust

	Löhe's *Proposal of a Union of Lutheran Christians for Apostolic Life*
1849	October 8: Establishment of the Lutheran diaspora and mission work, already in existence since 1841, as the *Gesellschaft für Innere Mission im Sinne der lutherische Kirche* [today, the Neuendettelsau Mission Society]
	From 1840 to 1860: Intensive contact with all German Lutheran free church mission starts and congregations; Löhe and the Mission Society stand with them to offer advice, support, and relief measures (Löhe: "midwives' service").
1850	June 19: First anniversary of the Mission Society in Nürnberg
1850	Founding of the fourth colony: Frankenhilf
	Since 1850: Publication of missionary tracts on doctrinal issues for Christians and congregations by the Mission Society, to fulfill their task of inner mission. These tracts achieve wide distribution and circulation.
	Publication of the *Correspondenzblatt* [Correspondence Letter] of the Mission Society (by Fr. Bauer and E. Stirner)
	January 1: First appearance of the *Freimundkalender*
1853	April 15: Relocation of the Mission Institute from Nürnberg to Neuendettelsau (headed by Friedrich Bauer)
	Commissioning of missionary Baierlein to the East Indies

	May 9: Founding of the *Diakonissenanstalt* [deaconess institute] (today, *Diakonie Neuendettelsau*)
1854	August 24: Founding of the Lutheran Iowa Synod in St. Sebald am Quell in Dubuque (by Neuendettelsau Lutherans Großmann, Deindörfer, Fritschel, Schüller)
1860	July 23: Native American missionary Moritz Bräuninger murdered near Powder River—first martyr of the Neuendettelsau Lutheran Mission
1861	Pastor Friedrich Wucherer—successor to Löhe as chairman of the Mission Society, 1861-1881
1864	Autumn: Destruction of the Native American mission station at Deercreek, Wyoming, by Native Americans during the American Civil War
1867	October 9: Dedication of the mission house (renovation of a purchased house)
1870	October 19: Dedication of the mission house (new construction)
1872	January 2: Death of Wilhelm Löhe

List of Sources

GW	*Gesammelte Werke Wilhelm Löhes*, Volumes 1–7 (in 12 separate volumes), published by Klaus Ganzert and Curt Schadewitz, on behalf of the Gesellschaft für Innere und Äußere Mission im Sinne der luth. Kirche, e.V. Neuendettelsau 1951–1986. Most citations are from this source.
GW.E	*GW.Ergaenzungsreihe*, Volume 1: Sermons on the Lord's Supper, 1866, published by Martin Wittenberg, Neuendettelsau, 1991. This contains an important collection of sermons not found in GW.
LStA	*Wilhelm Löhe—Studienausgabe*, published by Dietrich Blaufuß, Volume 1: Drei Bücher von der Kirche, 1845, Neuendettelsau, 2006. Scholarly new edition of GW 5, 83–179.
Deinzer	Deinzer, Johannes, *Wilhelm Löhes Leben*, Volumes 1–2 (4th edition), Neuendettelsau, 1935; Volume 3, Gütersloh, 1892.
Löhe Archive	Archive of the Gesellschaft für Innere und Äußerer Mission im Sinne der Lutherischen Kirche e.V. Neuendettelsau

Sources

Advent	GW 6.2, p. 18
	GW 6.3, p. 459
Christmas	Deinzer 3. 1892, pp. 234–235 (ca. 1870)
	GW 6.1, p. 36
	GW 6.3, pp. 463–464
New Year	GW 6.3, pp. 466–467
Epiphany	GW 6.3, pp. 468–470
	GW 6.3, p. 132
Invocavit	GW 6.2, pp. 194–196
Maundy Thursday	GW 6.2, pp. 242–243
Good Friday	GW 6.3, pp. 330–336
	GW 6.1, pp. 771–772
Easter	Sermon for Easter; manuscript in the Löhe Archive
	GW 6.3, pp. 498–499
	GW 6.2; pp. 399–400
	GW 6.3, p. 499
Ascension	GW 6.1, pp. 95–96
	GW 6.2, pp. 328–329
Pentecost	GW 6.3, pp. 445–446
	GW 6.3, pp. 514–515
Trinity	GW 6.3, p.779
	GW 6.3, pp. 527–528
Church Dedication Festival	Sermon for Church Dedication 1855; manuscript in the Löhe Archive
	GW 6.2, pp. 732–734
Festival of Harvest	GW 6.2, pp. 732–734

Festival of the Reformation	GW 6.2, pp. 179, 182–183
	GW 6.2, pp. 720–723
End of the Church Year	GW 6.2, p. 691
	GW 6.1, p. 193
God's Word	GW 3.1, pp. 38–39
	GW 5.1, pp. 150–151; LStA 1, pp. 144:22, 25–27 and 145:10–15, 19
	GW 5.1, pp. 109, 102, 103, 104; LStA 1, pp. 58:2–8, 44:5–14, 45:12–46:8, 47:18–48:15
	Festival of the Reformation 1849; manuscript in the Löhe Archive
Christian Faith	GW 6.3, p. 781 Pkt. 6.
	GW 6.1, pp. 674–675
Christian Prayer	GW 6.1, pp. 50–56
	GW 3.1, pp. 325, 326 and GW 5.1, p. 176; LStA 1, p. 200:3–7
	GW 7.1, pp. 14-15
Church Fellowship	GW 5.1, pp. 88–94, 96, 117–118, 124, 126, 130, 133, 135, 162–163; LStA 1, pp. 16:22–25, 17:8–10, 19:23–20:25, 23:9–19, 24:3–25:8, 26:3, 27:17–28:8, 32:1–19, 75:14–20, 76:2–5, 89:4–7, 92:20–25, 99:24–26, 105:1–3, 109:21–111:3, 170:3–12, 171:9–13
	GW 5.1, pp. 221–222 cp. edition 1848, p. 27, GW 5.2, p. 990 (1857).
The Church's Worship	GW 6.3, p. 199
	GW 5.1, p. 16, 177; LStA 1, pp. 200:7–9,

15–17, 22–24, 201:21–202:1
GW 7.1, p. 13
JBMLB 2, 1947, p. 78, from
Correspondenzblatt der Gesellschaft
17, 1866, pp. 37–44
GW.E 1, pp. 141:17–142:4
GW.E 1, p. 46:8–22
GW.E 1, p. 85:5–26

Regarding Creation Wedding sermon on Eph. 5:22ff, 1857 and from a manuscript dated April 25, 1866, in the Löhe Archive
Deinzer 3, p. 192
GW 2, pp. 26–27
GW 6.2, p. 664
GW 2, p. 29
Deinzer 1. (2) 1874, p. 218 ({4} 1935, p. 186ff.) and GW 6.1, p. 145 and GW 5.2, p. 1127 in footnote 233
GW 2, pp. 242, 323
GW 2, p. 446 Regest and Deinzer 2, pp. 183–184

Christian Hope Deinzer 2, p. 63; GW 6.1, p. 836 and GW 2, p. 275
Deinzer 2, p. 55
GW 6.1, selected from pp. 186–191
GW 6.1, p. 213
GW 6.1, pp. 704–705
GW 6.1, from pp. 192–193
Sermon on 1 Cor. 15:35ff; manuscript in the Löhe Archive
GW 6.2, pp. 669, 277
GW 6.2, p. 677
GW 6.1, p. 215
GW 6.2, p. 391
Letter; May 25, 1846, to S. G. Lieschin
GW 1, p. 743

GW 5.1, p. 90; LStA 1, p. 20:22–22
"Two Children's Lessons from Pastor Löhe";
    manuscript in the Löhe Archive
GW 6.1, p. 193.

Appendix
Löhe as Pastoral Theologian: The Discipline of the Shepherd

John T. Pless

Over twenty-five years ago, in what would prove to be a pivotal text in recovering pastoral theology as a genuinely churchly discipline rather than a clinical or managerial undertaking, Thomas Oden begins his *Pastoral Theology: Essentials of Ministry* with this definition of pastoral theology: "Because it is a pastoral discipline, pastoral theology seeks to join the *theoretical* with the practical. It is theoretical insofar as it seeks to develop a consistent theory of ministry, accountable to Scripture and tradition experientially sound and internally self-consistent. Yet it is not merely a theoretical statement or objective description of what occurs in ministry. It is also a *practical* discipline, for it is concerned with implementing concrete pastoral tasks rather than merely defining them. Its proximate goal is an improved theory of ministry. Its longer ranged goal is the improved practice of ministry."[1] Wilhelm Löhe's work certainly fits with Oden's description. In the midst of the religious, philosophical, and political turbulence of nineteenth-century Germany, the Bavarian cleric sought to articulate what he thought to be an improved doctrine of the office that he believed to be yet

---

1 Thomas Oden, *Pastoral Theology: Essentials of Ministry* (New York: Harper and Row, 1983), x–xi.

unfolding out of the New Testament. But Löhe's ultimate goal had to do with the practice of the care of souls.

From 1837 until his death in 1872, Löhe was pastor of the Nicolai Church in Neuendettelsau. This formed the context of his thinking. David Ratke observes, "Löhe's entire thought and perspective and life revolved around the axis that is the congregation. It is here that the apostolic Word comes to life; it is in the congregation that the church finds expression. Löhe did not emphasize praxis at the expense of dogma. To be sure, doctrine was the pillar of fire which guided the church during the dark nights of apostasy and the pillar of cloud during the days when everything seemed lost. But the impulse for Löhe's reflections was always the congregation and its life."[2] Löhe would forge his pastoral theology out of his own work as a preacher, liturgist, and pastor. Shaped by his childhood experiences in the village church at Fürth, university studies at Erlangen and Berlin, and several congregational assignments prior to his coming to Neuendettelsau, Löhe was drawn to reflection on the church's confession and life, the character and work of the pastor.

Löhe was the product of a pious Christian home. While his father, a successful merchant, died at the age of fifty-two when Löhe was only eight years old, his mother would exert a strong influence on her son's religious development. Barbara Löhe's own spiritual life was shaped by Johann Arndt's *Garden of Paradise* and J.F. Starck's *Daily Handbook*. Later, Löhe would reminisce on his mother's influence, saying that when his father died, "she did what she thought was right. Her love for the ministry and the church led her, although

---

2 David C. Ratke, *Confession and Mission, Word and Sacrament: The Ecclesial Theology of Wilhelm Löhe* (St. Louis: Concordia Publishing House, 2001), 55.

she was a widow, to let me choose such a life's calling. I owe her a thousand thanks. Who knows whether I would have become a Christian if I had not become a pastor."[3] Löhe also tells of how he would play church: "In our small yard where there was a chopping block, I gathered the children of the rent people who lived in our house, put on a black apron to serve as a gown, stepped onto the chopping block, which served as a pulpit, preached, sang, and prayed. Sometimes my mother would say to my father: 'A minister is lost in that boy if you don't let him study.'"[4] The piety of his parental home insulated young Löhe from the rationalism which would have been present in some degree in the village church and school. His confirmation day was particularly memorable. After completing his studies at the *Gymnasium* in nearby Nürnberg—where Löhe, under the influence of its rector Karl Louis Roth, would confirm his aspirations to become a pastor—he entered the University of Erlangen in November of 1826. Roth would have a similar impact upon J.W Hoefling, Adolph von Hareless, Christoph Luthardt, and J.C.K. von Hoffmann, all of whom studied at the *Gymnasium* and would eventually play prominent roles at Erlangen.

It is at Erlangen that Löhe began to develop a strong Lutheran consciousness, although his presence as a student there predates the Erlangen School which would develop in the coming decade. It was a Reformed preacher and adjunct professor at Erlangen, Christian Krafft, who would awaken in Löhe (as he would in von Hoffmann, von Harless, and others) an appreciation for the confessional character of

---

[3] Wilhelm Loehe, *Three Books About the Church*, trans. James Schaaf (Philadelphia: Fortress Press, 1969), 3.

[4] Hans Schwarz, *Theology in a Global Context: The Last Two Hundred Years* (Grand Rapids: Eerdmans, 2005), 92–93.

Lutheranism in contrast to most of the rest of the faculty who were still captivated by rationalism. Inspired not so much by Krafft's intellect as by his spirit, Löhe was led to read the theologians of seventeenth-century Lutheran Orthodoxy, especially David Hollaz, the last great dogmatician of that era. Löhe would follow his mentor in supporting the Basel Mission Society. It was not until 1842 that Löhe ceased supporting this group and instead sought to promote a confessionally-defined approach to missions.

In the summer of 1828, Löhe went to study in Berlin where both Hegel and Schleiermacher were lecturing. Löhe referred to his sojourn in Berlin as his "desert" and "Patmos." After attending a lecture by Hegel in Berlin, the young Löhe penned in his diary: "Understood nothing, nothing to understand." He was impressed by Schleiermacher's sermonic abilities, but not his theology. More positively, Löhe appreciated Ernst Wilhelm Hengstenberg, August J.W. Neander, Ludwig F.F. Theremin, and especially the practical theologian, Gerhard F.A. Strauß, whose example of an intense but churchly piety would leave its imprint on him. Löhe learned from Strauß to distinguish mysticism from pietism. In Strauß, Löhe found a teacher who awed him with a piety and romantic spiritual language that would correspond to his own religious instincts. In a letter dated 15 June 1828, Löhe wrote to his friend, H.W. E. Reichold, back in Erlangen: "Esteem high the evangelical simplicity! Give the small writings of Luther, as far as you can, to the members of the lower strata. So your circle will remain in blessing and the charge of mysticism will pass by. Do not encourage to make private hours of edification. Friends may pray together with friends, but everyone finds nourishment in our church, because the gospel is preached purely. I also desire that the mission circle deal less with prayer and singing, which have their place in home worship, in the church and otherwise, where one is together with those who belong to him, and instead read missionary reports and historical writings. The Bible is to be read but without explanations. I shall defend all this when I come back....Neither the lecture circle nor the missionary circle may be edification hours, but Christian conversation. Surely, this is edifying, too. You will agree with me, when I come. The *Pastorale* of Strauß, that I want to read and maybe dictate to you completely, has taught me much about the right distinction between mysticism and pietism from what is evangelical."[5] Both Berlin and Erlangen contributed to Löhe's shift from one who was a child of the Awakening to a self-consciously Lutheran identity. Yet the shift was not abrupt. On the day of his ordination on 25 July 1831, Löhe would write emphatically of his fidelity to the Lutheran Symbols. Three years later in 1834, he would still feel free to preach in a Reformed pulpit. Lothar Vogel observes that it was only in 1834-1835, when the church conflicts in Silesia heightened, that Löhe embraced the confessional understanding that would mark him a convinced Lutheran.[6]

In 1867, Gottfried Thomasius would write of his own movement from the Awakening to a more deeply Lutheran position through embracing justification of the sinner by grace through faith: "Thus we were Lutherans before we even knew it; without reflecting upon the confessional idiosyncrasy of our church, or upon the confessional differences which separate it from others, we were (Lutherans) in fact. We were not even thoroughly familiar with these differences. We read the symbolic books of the church as testimonies

---

5   Wilhelm Löhe, *Gesammelte Werke* (GW), ed. Klaus Ganzert (Neuendettelsau: Freimund Verlag, 1951–1986), I:270.
6   Lothar Vogel, "Awakening and Confessionalism: Wilhelm Löhe's Theological Teachers," unpublished lecture given at the meeting of the International Löhe Society in Neuendettelsau on 26 July 2008; 6.

of sound doctrine...but their symbolical significance concerned us little. But as soon as we began to realize that we were standing squarely in the middle of Lutheranism... so we became Lutherans, freely, from within."[7] Thomasius' testimony seems to fit Löhe as well. Like others who would be identified with the revival of confessional Lutheranism known as the Erlangen School, Löhe would read and be influenced by the writings of Johann Georg Hamann (1730-88).

After his ordination in 1831, Löhe served in several pastoral posts before beginning his work at Neuendettelsau on 1 August 1837. For a short time he would serve as a vicar to the aged pastor in his hometown of Fürth, Pastor Ebert. This ended unhappily with the older pastor exhibiting jealousy over his younger associate's popularity as a visitor of the sick and the elderly. Most significant was his service as a vicar from 20 October 1831 to 26 February 1834 in Kirchenlamitz. Here Löhe worked under Pastor Christian Sommer and was "confronted by a range of demands that, as he met them, shaped the basic lines of his future ministry."[8] It was here that Löhe developed as both a preacher and curate of souls. Yet it was his pastoral success that would generate conflict. A prominent judge in the congregation felt himself unduly attacked by Löhe's preaching. Charges were leveled against the young cleric, accusing him of holding forbidden conventicles. Löhe was charged with fostering "a debauching and pernicious mysticism by which you allow actions which lead to a disruption of familial and social order, the creation of a detrimental religious separatism, and a transformation

---

[7] Quoted by Hermann Sasse, "The Results of the Lutheran Awakening of the 19th Century—Part II," *Theological Quarterly* (October 1951), 244.

[8] Kennth F. Korby, *Theology of Pastoral Care in Wilhelm Loehe with Special Attention to the Function of the Liturgy and the Laity* (Fort Wayne: Concordia Theological Seminary Printshop, n.d.), 91.

of active Christianity into a dead, powerless, and lifeless religion of feeling."[9] Löhe was forced to leave Kirchenlamitz, relieved of his position by the Consistory. This was Löhe's first experience with church politics; it would not be his last.

After a string of temporary positions in Nürnberg and surrounding villages, Löhe applied for and was called to the pastorate of the Nicolai Church in Neuendettelsau. He married a former catechumen, Helene Andrae, six years to the day of his ordination, 25 July 1837. A week later, Löhe and his eighteen-year-old bride moved to Neuendettelsau, a village of about 500, where they would remain for the rest of their lives.

Six years later, Helene, only twenty-four years old, died from complications with the birth of their fourth child. Within a year, this infant son would also perish. Löhe would never get over his wife's death, and it would leave its mark on his piety and his work. In the writings that come after his wife's death, Löhe expresses something of a heavenly homesickness, a yearning for the consummation of the Christian community in the New Jerusalem. This is especially evident in his *Three Books About the Church*, published in 1845. The impact of Helene's death echoes throughout Löhe's life as he commemorates the anniversary of her death, November 24, yearly. In 1859, he includes a prayer for widowers in a prayer book that very much reflects his own loss: "O living God and Comforter of those who mourn, I have lost my dearest treasure on earth in childbirth. You have torn a rib and a piece of my heart from me. It is, however, your good will, Lord my God. You gave her to me and let her be with me for a short time and now she has been taken out of this misery back to you, because she knew and called upon your Son. Comfort me, a sad, miserable widower and help carry

---

9   Quoted by Schaaf in *Three Books About the Church*, 9–10.

this pain and raise my children and send a holy glimpse that I and my children can come together before you in a new joy and eternal love, which you plant in all marital love and can make all suffering eternal joy and goodwill. We praise you in eternity. Amen."[10]

The death of his wife was one of several deaths that impressed in Löhe a profound awareness of the shortness of this temporal life, stirring in him a sense of longing for the resurrection of the body and the communion of saints. He writes of his father's death: "On the day my father died, October 28, 1816—a Monday—I was in school. Our old servant, Susanna, came and got me. As I entered the room, my family was lying on their knees, praying for cessation of the painful struggle. Two of my sisters stood drowned in grief at the head and foot end of the death bed, respectively. My oldest sister, Anna, the sickly one, sat beside the stove without tears but with deep sobbing. As I entered the room, my mother rising from her prayers, took me by the hand and led me to my father, lying in his death rattle, put my hand in his and had me among other things which I don't remember anymore, promise that I would never be a disgrace to my previous father in his grave. Barely had I finished my promise when my father stopped breathing, and I was an orphan."[11] Seven of Löhe's twelve siblings died in infancy or childhood.

The vacuum created by the death of his wife was filled with even more intense devotion to pastoral work, theological writing, and the organization of missionary work and works of mercy. His reputation as a preacher grew beyond the confines of his parish, prompting some to call Löhe "the

---

10   Quoted by Ratke, 35.
11   Quoted by Theodor Schober, *Wilhem Loehe: Witness of the Living Lutheran Church*, trans. Sister Bertha Mueller (n.p., n.d), 5.

Chrysostom of his century." Löhe understood the Divine Service as the place where the heavenly Bridegroom meets His bride. He sought to recover the best liturgical practices of previous centuries so that the congregation need not be dressed in the threadbare worship forms of pietism and rationalism, but in the splendor that befits the bride of Christ. For Löhe, the center of the church was the liturgy of Word and Supper; from this lively and life-giving center, every aspect of the church's life, including pastoral care, radiated.

Kenneth Korby was of the opinion "that whoever wills to enter the thought of Wilhelm Löhe on the matter of the cure of souls must enter via his understanding of the church."[12] Noting that Löhe did not develop his views on the church systematically in the way of a classical dogmatics text, Korby echoed the observation of Walter Bouman that "his (Löhe') whole life and thought, his correspondence, his parish duties, his worldwide concerns revolved around the nature of the church so that a biography of him can at the same time be an ecclesiology."[13]

Three strands of Löhe's ecclesiological thinking relative to pastoral care emerge. First, there is the oneness of the church. Drawing on the epistle to the Ephesians and the creedal confession that "I believe in one holy Christian and apostolic Church," Löhe provides a corrective to the conceptuality of the church as "visible and invisible" inherited from Lutheran Orthodoxy and widely used in the nineteenth century.[14] Löhe did not abandon this distinction as can be

---

12   Korby, *Theology of Pastoral Care in Wilhelm Loehe*, 307.

13   *Ibid.*, 148.

14   See Heinrich Schmid, *Doctrinal Theology of the Evangelical Lutheran Church* trans. Charles A. Hay and Henry E. Jacobs (Minneapolis: Augsburg, 1961), 582–99 and Holsten Fagerberg, *Bekenntnis, Kirche, und Amt in der deutschen konfessionellen Theologie des Jahrhunderts* (Uppsala: Almqvist & Wiksells Boktryckeri, 1952), 127–131.

seen, among other places, in his *Agenda* of 1844 and his *Three Books About the Church*. In the foreword to the agenda, Löhe writes that the church is the "marvelous creation of her one and only Lord and Master, which has demonstrated and will demonstrate herself independent of everything except Word and Sacrament. In her totality the church is and remains invisible and appears visibly sometimes here, sometimes there, as her banners wave in the breeze sometimes here, sometimes there, and her marks appear in Word and Sacrament sometimes here, sometimes there."[15]

In attempting to maintain the confession that the church is one and to avoid positing two churches, one visible and the other invisible, Löhe seeks to speak of the church as simultaneously visible and invisible. This Löhe does by using the analogy of the human being who is both body and soul, one not existing without the other in this life, and by making a distinction between those who are "called" as those embraced in the visible church and those who are "chosen" as members of the invisible church.[16] Korby acknowledges that Löhe's treatment of the visible/invisible distinction is not without difficulties from the multiple perspectives of missiology, systematics, and pastoral care.[17] He identifies what he sees as problematic when one attempts to use the distinction: "To be caught in the tug of war initiated by the use of the words 'visible' and 'invisible' is to be threatened always to flee into the invisible, thereby turning every day churchly life over to machinations, devices, techniques, and powers of all sorts. Or, to choose to concentrate on that reality that corresponds to 'visible' is to shift the understanding of the Word of God and faith so that the inner life of the

---

15 Cited in Korby, *Theology of Pastoral Care in Wilhelm Loehe*, 178.
16 Loehe, *Three Books About the Church*, 87–89.
17 Korby, *Theology of Pastoral Care in Wilhelm Loehe*, 180–181.

church is drained off into the quagmires of experientialism and into the legalisms of righteousness by works or rituals. And yet, to hold to both terms 'visible' and 'invisible' is very nearly to be caught defenseless against the 'two church solution' that has so often threatened the church's unity and the Gospel."[18] Yet, positively, Korby argues that Löhe is able to escape turning the doctrine of the church into an abstraction by avoiding a shift from oral/auditory images to visual ones in his ecclesiology. The inner life of the church which is hidden is given outward expression in preaching, baptizing, absolving, and distributing the Lord's Supper.

The inner and outer life of the church is joined together in a unity not to be broken. Löhe writes in his *Three Books About the Church*: "In short, the visible church is the tabernacle of God among men, and outside it there is no salvation. A man separates himself from God the Father if he separates himself from the church, his mother....As a man stands in relation to the church, so he stands in relation to his God."[19]

Second, the apostolic character of the church means that the church is not a static institution but a living organism. The church is both called and calling. By the apostolic Word, that is, the living voice of preaching that is in conformity to the apostolic Scriptures, the church is called to life in Christ Jesus.[20] This is the calling to faith as faith comes from hear-

---

18   *Ibid.*, 182–183.
19   Loehe, *Three Books About the Church*, 90.
20   Korby expresses the connection between the apostolic Word and mission: "As the mission is the church of God in motion, so the energy of that motion is the Word of God, the apostolic Word. That Word alone is the energy; that Word alone is the uniting center. It is not the constitutional order of the church, not a lord, not a bishop that is the uniting power in the center of the church, but this apostolic Word, the Scripture. Apostolic is the principle name for the church, for these clear Scriptures are not only the uniting word, but that clear Word that is always at the center and the church is never without 'its glorious center.' Loehe equates the apostolic Word and the Scriptures. However, at the same

ing the Gospel. The church that is apostolic is constituted in and by this faith-creating Word. At the same time, the church that is apostolic is a calling church, as this church confesses Christ before the world and through the preaching of Christ gathers people from every tribe and tongue into the holy community whose head and center is the Lamb of God.

Acts 2:42 ("And they devoted themselves to the apostles' teaching and fellowship, to the breaking of bread and the prayers") is crucial in Löhe's thinking on the nature of the life of the apostolic congregation expressed in worship. Löhe's use of this pericope is another example of his avoidance of abstractions as he concretely describes the character of the liturgical congregation as praying, preaching, and celebrating the Lord's Supper.[21]

Gathered by the apostolic Word, the church is fed by the body and blood of the Lord in the Holy Supper. While the appearance of the four items noted in Acts 2:42 might appear in varying degrees in different gatherings of the congregation for worship, all four come to culmination and union in the service of Holy Communion. "One element may be appropriately stressed over the others in any given gathering. But the great high point, the fountain of all other life and worship, is the union of the four elements. That union is the celebration of Holy Communion."[22]

The Sacrament of the Altar shaped Löhe's understanding of the church as a living organism. The church is known

---

time he continues to keep alive the quality of the Word as spoken, as oral." *Theology of Pastoral Care in Wilhelm Loehe*, 177.

21   *Ibid.*, 170. Also see Kenneth Korby, "Wilhelm Loehe and Liturgical Renewal" in *The Lutheran Historical Conference: Essays and Reports 1972* (St. Louis: Lutheran Historical Conference, 1974), where Korby traces how Loehe develops the use of Acts 2:42 in his *Laienagende* of 1852 (71).

22   Korby, *Theology of Pastoral Care in Wilhelm Loehe*, 170.

from the altar. And it is from the altar that mission is generated and to the altar that mission returns. The movement of mission is from and to the altar as the church lives as "an organism of rescuing love."

Contrary to interpretations of Löhe that would see in him a hierarchal clericalism that demeaned the life of the laity, *disenfranchising* them from the life of the church, there is in Löhe a unity between the holy office and the holy priesthood. Both are from the Lord. The office is established by Christ for the sake of the apostolic Word so that it might be heard, believed, and confessed in the places where the priestly people called by the Lord live and work.[23] In his own way, Löhe revitalizes a Lutheran doctrine of vocation that enlivens the laity to live out their callings in the world, especially in the Christian home where the Word of Christ is to dwell richly. Thus the laity are not only the objects of spiritual care, they are engaged in this work in union with the pastor. Korby observes that Löhe's "*Haus-Schul-und Kirchenbuch* proved to be a coherent statement expressing the union of the home, the school, and the church in mutual care of souls, and it included valuable guidance for laymen to engage directly in that caring work."[24]

Third, the Lutheran Church is a confessional communion. As an heir of the confessional reawakening of the nineteenth century, Löhe embraced the Lutheran Confessions as the clear exposition of the Holy Scriptures. This led him to reject the Prussian Union and all that it entailed. Löhe's confessionalism may be described as a "sacramental confessionalism" in that he understood all of Lutheran

---

23 See Kenneth Korby, "The Pastoral Office and the Priesthood of Believers" in *Lord Jesus Christ, Will You Not Stay: Essays in Honor of Ronald Feuerhahn on the Occasion of His Sixty-fifth Birthday,* edited by J. Bart Day et al (Houston: The Feuerhahn Festschrift Committee, 2002), 333–371.

24 Korby, *Theology of Pastoral Care in Wilhelm Loehe,* 173.

doctrine drawn together in the sacrament of the altar. This sacramental confessionalism had both ecclesiological and pastoral consequences. Ecclesiastically, it meant that for Löhe there could be no intercommunion with those of another confession. Pastorally, it meant that the Confessions are embraced to keep the Lutheran Church centered in the purity of evangelical proclamation and administration of the Lord's Supper. For Löhe, the Confessions prevented involvement in inter-confessional mission societies and the embrace of what he identified as "methodistic" tactics of evangelization and pastoral care.

For Löhe the ecclesiological foundation of pastoral theology would shape the practice of the care of souls in several ways. First, the care of souls properly belongs to the church. Korby writes, "The shape of Löhe's pastoral theology can be designated as a tri-polar field. The basic pole is the Word of God; the other two poles are the congregation and the pastor. As the Spirit leads the congregation, giving them pastors and teachers as gifts, the same spirit gives the *means* for the church's life and work. The wisdom and power of the pastoral office lie in the use of that Word. The object of pastoral care is the creation of new creatures. In *Seelsorge*, therefore, God's Word, not human skills, is the essence of persuasion, for the aim of the Spirit is to make a new and holy people, not merely to modify behavior with human persuasion. Care of souls is the cure of souls."[25]

Set within the church is the holy office. It is through this office that Christ serves His bride. Löhe understands the pastor to be in succession with the apostles not by attachment to place or continuity of persons but by means of a common doctrine. Ordination places a man in the office

---

25 Kenneth Korby, "Loehe's *Seelsorge* for his Fellow Lutherans in America," *Concordia Historical Institute Quarterly* 45 (November 1972), 235.

which Christ instituted. For Löhe the ministry is derived from neither the congregation nor the episcopacy; it is established by the risen Lord with the sending of the apostles.

Löhe sees that the office of the keys is given to the whole church but only ministers are entrusted with the responsibility to exercise the keys in loosing and binding sin. Rudolf Keller has pointed to Löhe's reliance on Andreas Osiander and the Brandenburg-Nurnberg church order at this point.[26] The minister does not serve by his own personal or charismatic authority, but by the mandate of Christ. Ordination, for Löhe, binds the minister to this mandate rather than the whims of the congregation. Löhe deals explicitly with the nature and authority of the office in his *Aphorisms* (1849 and 1851). In his *Der Evangelische Geistliche* (two volumes;1852-1858) he explores various facets of the pastor's life and work, both in terms of his character and the skills needed for shepherding and teaching.

Second, Löhe insists on the primacy of private confession and absolution in pastoral care: "Private confession is the mother of all care of souls and for it there is no substitute."[27] An evangelical reclaiming of confession and absolution is anchored in the chief article, justification by faith alone. Absolution is the enactment of the justifying word of the Gospel. For Löhe the *Beichtvater*, or father confessor, is not a judge over the penitent but a servant or ambassador who is sent with the verdict of the judge: forgiveness to those broken by their sin.

Gerhard von Zezschwitz, a professor of practical theology at Erlangen who had Löhe as his father confessor, said that

---

26   Rudolf Keller, "Reformatorische Wurzekn der Amtslehre von Wilhelm Löhe," in *Unter einem Christus sein und straiten: Festschrift zum 70. Geburtstag von Friedrich Wilhelm Hopf, D.D.* eds. Jobst Schöne and Volker Stolle (Erlangen: Verlag der Evangelisch-Lutherischen Mission, 1980), 118.

27   GW IV:83.

only he who knows Löhe as a Seelsorger and father confessor really knows him fully.[28] Already in the pre-Neuendettelsau years, Löhe identified confession as more important for man's eternal welfare than sowing and harvesting is for his temporal well-being.[29] An 1835 draft of what would be published two years later as his *Communion Booklet* spoke of the blessing and power of private confession. In 1843, six years after Löhe's coming to Neuendettelsau, private confession emerged as a regular practice in the congregation. Three years later, in 1846, Löhe absolved 153 communicants in a single day.[30] Wolfhart Schlichting indicates that Löhe heard 2,250 individual confessions in 1858.[31]

Löhe believed that the practice of general confession should be retained for weighty pastoral reasons. Private confession is to be urged not as a replacement for the general confession but as a means that makes it possible for the penitent to name specific sins and the pastor to provide spiritual care—exploration, examination, and absolution—appropriate to the condition of the penitent. Löhe gives guidance as to how confession is to be made so that it avoids what he calls a shameless rambling on about sin and its effects or a confession of one's circumstances, but rather a naming of the sin before God. While private confession gives the pastor opportunity to counsel the penitent in the avoidance of new

---

28 Martin Wittenberg, "Wilhelm Löhe and Confession: A Contribution to the History of Seelsorge and the Office of the Ministry," in *And Let Every Tongue Confess: Essays in Honor of Norman Nagel on the Occasion of His Sixty-fifth Birthday* eds. Gerald Krispin and Jon Vieker (Dearborn, Michigan: Nagel Festschrift Committee, 1990), 119; also see Stephen van der Hoek, "The Unique Contribution of Wilhelm Löhe to the Renewal of the Practice of Private Confession," *Lutheran Theological Journal* (August 2008), 100–108.

29 *Ibid.*, 120.

30 *Ibid.*, 122.

31 Wolfhart Schlichting, "Löhe" in *Theologische Realenzyklopädie* Band 21ed. Gerhard Müller (Berlin: Walter de Gruyter, 1991), 411.

sins, Löhe praises confession as God's own way of humbling and mortifying the old Adam. Only the one whose bones have been crushed by the Law is in a position to hear the words of absolution that restore broken sinners to joy and gladness.

Third, tied to the restoration of confession and absolution is the necessity of discipline within the church. The word of blessing in the absolution directed toward sinners who repent has its antithesis in the word of curse in the binding key spoken to hardened sinners who will not repent. Korby writes, "Löhe saw private confession and absolution as only a half measure if there is not joined with it the power to refuse absolution or to deny the Lord's Supper. To use only one key means the loss of both. Löhe judged easy or cheap care of souls to be worthless. 'There is no such thing as care of souls without training or discipline.' If there is no practice of excommunication, absolution loses some of its significance."[32] For Löhe, discipline in the church is work of rescue. It may be compared to the physician setting a broken bone—painful but necessary for the healing of the patient. The binding key is necessary so that finally the loosing key can be employed to set free the person brought to repentance.

On more than one occasion, Löhe's insistence on church discipline would get him in trouble. For example, in 1860, he refused to officiate at a wedding of a member who had divorced his wife. The state through the Bavarian church insisted that Löhe perform the wedding or else be suspended from his pastorate. Löhe refused and was suspended for a time. This episode is illustrative of Löhe's ongoing worry that a territorial church made church discipline nearly impossible. It was a worry that more than once prompted

---

32   Korby, *Theology of Pastoral Care in Wilhelm Loehe*, 189.

him to seriously ponder leaving the territorial church for a free church.

Fourth, sermon, sacrament, and catechization form a necessary triad in the care of souls. In *Three Books About the Church*, Löhe characterized his own time as "a time of one-sidedness and experimentation."[33] Writing in a time of liturgical experimentation and exploration of new paradigms for mission and ministry, Korby noted the parallels between Löhe's time and the late twentieth century in regard to what he believed was detrimental to the genuine care of souls. The care of souls requires church; that is, the care of souls is dependent on a context formed by preaching, the Lord's Supper, and catechetical instruction.

Löhe was himself a gifted preacher who possessed an extraordinary power of speech, energy of expression, pictorial richness, and passion grounded in deep conviction.[34] His preaching followed the traditional lectionary, and he suggested that the Lutheran preacher not replace it with free texts or with continuous readings from Holy Scripture. Instead, Löhe writes that "a man who changes texts every year is no good as a preacher for the people, or we might say for the church."[35] For Löhe, the preacher grows deeper in the text as he expounds the same well-known pericopes year after year.

Löhe understood the preacher as an ambassador of divine reconciliation who speaks with sincerity and forthrightness as one who is sent. The preacher does not need to decorate his proclamation with literary artfulness. As in pastoral care,

---

33 Loehe, *Three Books About the Church*, 173.
34 See Erika Gieger, *Wilhelm Löhe 1808–1872: Leben—Werk—Wirkung* (Neuendettelsau: Freimund Verlag, 2003), 29. The standard work on Löhe's preaching remains Hans Kreßel, *Wilhelm Löhe als Prediger* (Gütersloh: C. Bertelsmann Verlag, 1929).
35 Loehe, *Three Books About the Church*, 169.

so also preaching is not given to the "new measures" of the Methodists, as he calls them, but to a confident reliance on the biblical Word. Thus, Löhe says that "A sincere preacher therefore will not intentionally withdraw himself nor intentionally make himself prominent, but he comes with the Word and the Word comes with him. He is a simple, faithful witness to the Word, and the Word witnesses to him—he and the Word appear as one. All his preaching is based on holy calm. Even when he condemns and the zeal of God's house consumes him, it is not the wrath of the warlike world but the wrath of the invulnerable, peace-loving God which is kindled in him. It is not primarily he who speaks but the Lord who speaks in him and through him, and the way he performs his duty is worthy of the Lord. Always it is the measure of manliness and maturity which distinguishes the preacher of the church."[36] Hugh Oliphant Old describes Löhe's preaching as "doxological" in that his sermons not only exhort congregants to adoration and worship but are in and of themselves hymns of praise as they draw the congregation into the angelic hymn.[37]

While his preaching was doxological, it could also be sharp and stern. Sins known to the public in Neuendettelsau such as drunkenness and immorality were named. On one occasion, Löhe preached a funeral sermon for a woman who had borne eight children with a man to whom she was never married. Löhe had cared for the woman on her death bed; she confessed her sin and received absolution and Holy Communion. Nevertheless, Löhe referred to her in the funeral sermon as "this poor whore," warning the

---

36   *Ibid.*, 168.
37   Hughes Oliphant Old, *The Reading and Preaching of the Scriptures in the Worship of the Christian Church*. Volume 6: The Modern Age (Grand Rapids: Eerdmans, 2007), 122–123.

congregation to avoid her sinful ways even as he rejoiced in her repentance.[38]

Preaching, for Löhe, does not aim to excite the emotions of the hearers but to implant in their inmost being the living and active Word which grows, as he says, like a mustard seed. Good preaching brings about patient perseverance with the Word and in the Word. Preaching requires of the preacher careful study, contemplation, and meditation so that the preacher might learn what Löhe identifies as "the great secret of preaching," namely that a preacher uses "what is familiar to create an entrance for the unfamiliar and to expound all the doctrines of the church on the basis of the texts which are familiar to all."[39]

Löhe's preparation for preaching was disciplined study and prayer. He typically began each day, Monday through Saturday, at 5:00 a.m. with study of the text. "I must give birth to my sermons with pain....I groan, pray, and am fearful till I step into the pulpit, and then God's grace is renewed."[40] Generally, his sermons were carefully written out word for word except for funeral sermons that were generally done in outline form. Hermann Bezzel, perhaps Löhe's most prominent successor, would say, "Löhe's sermons are nothing less than a reflection of the thoughts of God."[41]

The sermon is linked to the sacrament. While Löhe writes of preaching that "among the means which the church uses for the salvation of souls, preaching occupies the first place,"[42] he sees the sermon as necessarily moving to the sacrament. As Thomas Schattauer observes, "For Löhe, the

---

38 Johannes Deinzer, *Wilhelm Löhes Leben,* vol. 2 (Nuremberg: Gütersloh, 1872–1892), 188.
39 Loehe, *Three Books About the Church,* 169.
40 Schober, *Wilhelm Loehe,* 85.
41 *Ibid.,* 87.
42 Loehe, *Three Books About the Church,* 167.

Lord's Supper provided a comprehensive interpretation of Christian existence."[43] This can be seen in an 1853 sermon on 1 Corinthians 5:6-8 where Löhe proclaims, "For Christians, the whole time from the sacrifice at Golgotha until the return of the Lord is a true and unceasing Easter celebration, a time of the Paschal Lamb and the Lord's Supper, not only in a figurative and symbolic way, but in a most perfect and holiest solemnity. New Testament congregations live from the preparation to the partaking of the Paschal Lamb, from partaking to preparation: between preparation and partaking time passes, until he comes. Ever anew they desire to partake of their eternal salvation in the Lamb of God who was slain and to be assured thereby full peace and joy in the Holy Spirit, full light and power for sanctification. There is no higher view of earthly life than this—and therefore no more perfect blossom of earthly life, no more time which deserves the name 'high time' than the time when one comes to the holy Supper and partakes of the Paschal Lamb. To celebrate the Lord's Supper—indeed, that is the highest, most glorious work of a Christian congregation—or rather, not a work, but where it lays down every work, where it lives entirely by faith"[44] (Rule of Prayer, 251-52). The Lord's Supper, according to Löhe, the energies inherent in the body and blood of Christ, enliven faith and love in the Christian individually and the church corporeally. Eating the body of Christ and drinking His blood, the church is most profoundly the Body of Christ.

Löhe sees the Lord's Supper as the ultimate gift of Christ Jesus, for here the Lamb of God imparts His body and blood

---

43 Thomas Schattauer, "The Reconstruction of Rite: The Liturgical Legacy of Wilhelm Löhe," *Rule of Faith, Rule of Prayer: Essays in Honor of Aidan Kavanagh*, eds. Nathan Mitchell and John Baldovin (Collegeville, Minnesota: The Liturgical Press, 1996), 251.

44 GW 5/2: 673

for the forgiveness of sins. With this gift the communicants are bound together with their Lord and with one another. At the altar, doctrine and life converge in Löhe's thinking. Contradiction of Christ's words must be laid aside; therefore, there could be no altar fellowship with those who twist or deny the Lutheran teaching. But Löhe held that there was more to the sacrament than simply having a correct doctrinal definition. Later in his life, addressing a pastoral conference in 1865, he says, "I am the same good Lutheran as earlier, but in a more profound way. Before, Lutheranism was for me little more than affirmation of the confessions from A-Z; now the whole of Lutheranism is for me hidden in the sacrament of the altar, in which, as can be shown, all the chief doctrines of Christianity, especially those of the Reformation, have their center and focus. The essential thing for me now is not so much the Lutheran doctrine of the Lord's Supper, but sacramental life and experience of the blessing of the sacrament possible only through partaking of it abundantly. The words 'sacramental Lutheranism' signify my advance."[45]

The benefits of the sacrament are to be preached. The Lord's Supper was honored by frequent, reverent, and salutary use in the congregation. Preparatory services on Friday and Saturday prior to communion Sundays aimed to assist Christians in a beneficial partaking of the sacred body and blood. Löhe also prepared a variety of devotional aids to help communicants examine themselves and meditate on the benefits of the sacrament. Löhe promoted a more frequent celebration of the sacrament in Neuendettelsau, moving beyond the traditional spring and fall communions with several services in the spring beginning with Palm

---

[45] Quoted in Thomas Schattauer, "Sunday Worship at Neuendettelsau Under Wilhelm Löhe," *Worship* (July 1985), 371.

Sunday and continuing through the Easter Season. In the autumn, there would be multiple services in October and November although parishioners typically communed only once during each cycle. In the 1850s, the pattern changed to the celebration of the Lord's Supper every three weeks and on major feast days. In the 1860s, Löhe established "small communion" services, abbreviated celebrations held early on the morning of those Sundays when there was no celebration of the sacrament in the main service.[46]

Catechization is necessary for a fruitful hearing of God's Word and a holy reception of the Lord's Supper. Löhe lauds Luther's Small Catechism as a confession of the Evangelical Lutheran Church, asserting that "no catechism in the world but this can be prayed."[47] He recognizes Luther's genius in crafting with such simplicity of style and yet richness of meaning. In *Three Books About the Church*, Löhe warns pastors against using the Catechism as a pretext for delivering dogmatic monologues and instead urges that the catechist stick to the words of the Catechism itself. He draws attention to Luther's own prefaces to the Small and Large Catechism as providing a simple and churchly method of teaching the faith. In this way, Löhe argues "the Catechism should be engraved on the memory of the child for its entire life."[48] He suggested that catechization move from the text to an exposition of its meaning to the clarification of its content for doctrine and life.

Fifth, Löhe maintains the necessity of making a distinction between the "ordinary" and "extraordinary"

---

[46] See Schattauer, "Sunday Worship at Neuendettelsau Under Wilhelm Löhe", 370–384. Also see Hans Kreßel, *Wilhelm Löhe als Liturg und Liturgiker* (Neuendettelsau: Freimund Verlag, 1952), 114–64.
[47] Loehe, *Three Books About the Church*, 171.
[48] GW VII/2:590.

forms of pastoral care.[49] The ordinary means for the care of souls are sermon, liturgy, and catechesis. The extraordinary means would be those pastoral activities that attend to specific needs and crises in the lives of believers. Here again we see that the church is fundamental to pastoral care. Korby writes, "So radical was this contextual setting to be understood that Löhe argued: if one does not anchor the extraordinary means in this general setting of the ordinary, he will make the grave error of turning the extraordinary into the ordinary. That is, the private care, the care of the individual, will become the ordinary means of the pastor's work and preaching, catechesis, and liturgy will become occasional, peripheral, and insignificant. The private care of the individual is extraordinary, by Löhe's description. But if it is to be fruitful and blessed work, it must be done with those on whom the ordinary means of the care of souls have done their work."[50]

Löhe spotted a tendency to replace the ordinary with extraordinary: "Such an inversion is what he (Löhe) called 'methodism' in pastoral care. Löhe called this a one-sidedness, growing out of the conviction that the Word of God would work effectively only if it were used in a certain way. By the attempt to achieve something special, something spectacular in this way was like cutting with the handle of a knife. The feverish creation of new measures for pastoral care will, in the long run, produce just that, 'new measures.' It does not take too long before the effects once produced by the 'new measures' begin to wear off, for in becoming the ordinary means for the care of souls, the extraordinary means do not have the staying power that the ordinary means contain

---

49   Loehe, *Three Books About the Church*, 245; also see Kenneth Korby, "Loehe's *Seelsorge* for his Fellow Lutherans in America," 227–246.

50   *Ibid.*, 246.

within themselves."⁵¹ Pastoral care for Löhe does not seek after the "new measures" with the multiplicity of techniques but the "old means" in their evangelical simplicity.

Sixth, intercessory prayer is a necessary component. "There is no care of souls without intercession and common prayer."⁵² The hallowing Word of God anchors the prayers of Christians in the gracious will of the Father. The General Prayer in the Divine Service is the priestly voice of the church making intercession for the world according to the apostolic mandate. Löhe sees that the Litany especially lends itself to intercession as it provides both structure and elasticity in bringing before God the needs of the sick and dying, the tempted and distressed, expectant mothers and widows; in short, it is expansive enough to incorporate all who need our prayers. Löhe composed *Seed Grains*, for example, to assist the laity in hallowing all of life by the Word of God and prayer. Löhe was known for his prayer books and devotional literature but also for his fervent prayers made at the bedside of the sick and the dying and in the presence of the tormented and spiritually distressed. Hans Schwarz observes the similarities between Löhe and his contemporary with whom he was acquainted, Johann Christoph Blumhardt (1805–80), in this respect.⁵³

When Löhe died in January of 1872, he left behind a legacy that would extend far beyond the little village of Neuendettelsau, the seat of his life's work. His contributions to missions and diaconal work remain and are rightly celebrated. His contributions to pastoral theology have often been eclipsed by approaches derived from psychological

---

51 *Ibid.*, 247.
52 GW VII/2:590.
53 Hans Schwarz, "Wilhelm Loehe in the Context of the Nineteenth Century," *Currents in Theology and Mission* (April 2006), 94

disciplines. In recent times—that is, within the last fifty years—the only pastoral theology in English, at least that utilizes Löhe, is the Barthian Eduard Thurneysen's *A Theology of Pastoral Care*.[54] We would do well to listen again to the wisdom of Löhe's pastoral theology, to critically engage his thought toward a renewed understanding and practice of the care of souls in our spiritually needy world.

---

54   Eduard Thurneysen, *A Theology of Pastoral Care*, trans. Jack A. Worthington and Thomas Wieser (Richmond: John Knox Press, 1962). In addition to the previously cited works of Kenneth F. Korby there is Hans Kreßel's important study, *Wilhelm Löhe als Katechet und als Seelsorger* (Neuendettelsau: Freimund Verlag, 1955) and Armin Wenz, "Ministry and Pastoral Theology of Löhe and Vilmar," *Logia* (Holy Trinity 2007), 15–24.

www.ingramcontent.com/pod-product-compliance
Lightning Source LLC
Chambersburg PA
CBHW070053120526
44588CB00033B/1413